ALSO BY JANET HAMILL

REAL FIRE

KNOCK

TALES FROM THE ETERNAL CAFÉ

BODY OF WATER

LOST CEILINGS

NOSTALGIA OF THE INFINITE

THE TEMPLE

TROUBLANTE

A MAP OF THE HEAVENS

SELECTED POEMS 1975-2017

JANET HAMILL

Spuyten Duyvil
New York City

The cover illustration is a replica of the author's current copy of National Geographic's 1957 poster of The Map of the Heavens. The author's copy of an original 1957 edition of the map, addressed on p. 86, found in a flea market in Englishtown, NJ in 1971, was too fragile to photograph. All the other photos were taken by the author of her study.

Library of Congress Cataloging-in-Publication Data

Names: Hamill, Janet, author.
Title: A map of the heavens : selected poems / Janet Hamill.
Description: New York City : Spuyten Duyvil, [2020]
Identifiers: LCCN 2019040023 | ISBN 9781949966695 (paperback)
Classification: LCC PS3558.A4219 A6 2020 | DDC 811/.54--dc23
LC record available at https://lccn.loc.gov/2019040023

CONTENTS

FOREWORD
PATTI SMITH

Some day she will find something to rest on. The waves will bring an oracle. Walking into the surf in her Venusian skirts. A voice of wind and thunder will tell her where to go.

—from *Worlds of Time*

A young girl with a mystical bend explores the vast arrangement of the stars. She looks toward the heavens for angels, a sense of her own destiny. She becomes a cartographer of sorts, shaping constellations of her own, mapping the sky with words.

We were not yet twenty when we met, and though much time has past, I can still picture us. She with her cropped hair and boatneck shirt and myself in school-girl black, reveling in literature, fashion, and rock n' roll. We shared our evolving hopes and the thrust of personal wounds, buoying one another in hard times, staying close as she navigated the dark wake of the unexpected loss of her mother.

Above all, poetry was our common bond, our great constant. I wrote of Medea; she penned the sweeping call of the Argonauts. We read the works of one another aloud, examined and encouraged. We befriended a pantheon of the venerated dead, literati through the ages. We wrote, danced and dreamed, magnifying their imagined presence. Our aspirations soared and we were never bored.

Her desk was piled with books. She embraced poets from Baudelaire to Dylan Thomas to Hart Crane. Yet she was drawn to the physical poetry of Jeanne Moreau and Fellini, the aesthetic yoke of Catholicism, and the mystery of travel. Eventually she left for parts unknown. Spain to Morocco to Harar to the Southwest to Hollywood. Wondrous landscapes providing the unique topography of her writing.

To read her work is to travel above the land and below the surface of the skin. Possessing a sensuality of narrative, her tales transport one through time, mixing historic and mythological drama. Her poems are intensely visual and musical, wrenching arias juxtaposed with scientific calm. Tones of bells, tones of color, brush strokes and heartquakes. A personal favorite of mine, "The Lonesome Death of H. Crane" reads like a film, lingering like *Knife in the Water*.

Through one century to the next, I have never ceased to admire her steadfast commitment, her ever unfolding body of work and the sacrifices laid upon the altar of her predestined vocation. Janet Hamill was a poet at eighteen, at twenty-eight, at sixty, and shall always be. Even in sleep, I imagine her hand reaching for a pen. I imagine the humble yet magnanimous cartographer mapping another spiraling constellation, an epiphany of words, experimental and divine.

INTRODUCTION
BOB HOLMAN

Janet Hamill, homegrown surrealist, Trance Poet, true American original. She is also a painter of pocket-sized paintings that display the constellations drifting in outer space—mine has a gorgeous gold frame that seems part of the painting. Now imagine her fronting Lost Ceilings, the garage band that took its name from one of her books, blending her cosmic imagery with roots rock'n'roll. Renaissance woman in the guise of a mild-mannered librarian; her life has been her art.

And her books! Travel guides via metaphysics. We traverse the world with her, then realize somehow the world is growing larger, at which point she writes those poems too, guided by a Moving Star, by Lost Ceilings, and now, this volume, the selected poems, *A Map of the Heavens*. Welcome to the Cosmos. It's made of words, as Muriel Rukeyser once wrote. Poetry's Twilight Zone. Welcome to the poetry of Janet Hamill.

There's a marvelous chaos in US poetics right now. Whole lineages lie buried beneath the information avalanche available via digital consciousness. And then there's the MFA certification system, its Ponzi scheme-like growth and instant karma. But Hamill's singular voice is one that very few taxonomies acknowledge. Let's hope this volume, containing poems from all seven of her poetry volumes, will rectify this unfortunate situation. To facilitate that, I suggest we head back to the days of downtown Manhattan in the 70s, when poets were majoring in community and hanging out in extremis, when the Beats, Umbra, Deep Image and New York School poets roamed the streets.

I think the first time I heard Janet perform her poetry was at the cast party for *The Cause of Gravity*, the first of four plays that Bob Rosenthal and I would write and stage. We were in Ray Gaspard's loft on the Bowery, just below Houston, Derelict Row, a block from where the Bowery Poetry Club is now, just below today's Whole Foods and Chinatown Y. Back then it was flophouses and Bowery bums, as they were called then, whiling the hours at quarter beer joints, or whatever the category below "dive bars" is.

This was, as I say, the early 70s, and Ray was pioneering the importation of reggae and all that goes with it, and the actor who played the Abominable Snowman in *The Cause*, like Ray and me a recent Columbia grad, Duane Tucker, streaked the party. No one noticed. Janet was a laser of attention in the kitchen as the revels swirled and shivered to a stop around her. No book, no paper—no one memorized their poems back then. Janet did. She flung back her head, closed her eyes and we were off. Not by volume, not by force—it was her singular focus magnetized our attention, her voice a pulsing, mesmerizing music. Her words spin out a web, a ladder to the night sky and all of us a single breath achieve lift off as silent slo-mo rocket and head out on a little exploratory intergalactic jaunt to far-flung galaxies. Poem as map, poet as captain. Now you can find your way to the ends of the universe by reading this *Map of the Heavens*. But then it was the time of *Troublante*, her first book, and she, and her poems, were radical, new, and available only through her spoken, chanted, entrancing voice.

Trance. By trance I don't mean that Janet goes into a trance, or that we the audience are induced into a hypnotic state. I mean both, *lo mismo*, the same, *Troublante*. The repetition of that name, the Trickster Instigator, the Beloved, the What That Makes Things Happen—what does it mean? The sound chant of it, that's what it "means." It pulls you in, it stops the world, it creates a world, poetry like we'd never heard before. The chant-hum-drone of it.

Here we were, hippies in black leather jackets. Cool. Hot. Fresh out of college. For Janet that was Glassboro State College, in Glassboro, NJ. That's where Janet turned her buddy Patti on to poetry, Patti being Patti Smith, and changed the course of US culture.

I'm trying to set a scene here, the scene of a scene. When I was making *The United States of Poetry* for PBS, I divvied up the country's poets by aesthetic, and the only other "Trance School" poet in the country I could come up with was Wanda Coleman. And as different as the poetry of Coleman and Hamill are, when they take off in performance, you take off with them—they are looking back at you from a different plane and will take you there if your ears are clear enough to hear the ancient vocal vibrations, hypnotic transcendence, poetry-into-music meld.

And as her voice carries you off, Hamill's books also travel, to far-flung reaches, to the deserts and cheap hotels, to the rundown temples and bohemian sideshows. Even though she never spent much time there, *Troublante* is Mexico incarnate. As she wrote me, "A reverie. I was back in NY after a year and a half in California. I'd made a few trips into Baja. Camping. Back in NY, I got a job working at the Museum of Natural History. I was in my glory. I'd been transformed by Jerry [Rothenberg]'s *Technicians [of the Sacred]* in CA. I was totally immersing myself in indigenous American cultures. In San Francisco, I'd devoured book on book on the North American tribes. Back in NY, I discovered the Latin American poets. I went nuts. The Museum was pre-Columbian heaven for artifacts. At home it was Neruda, Paz and Borges. Those were the primary influences then."

Hearing *Troublante*, I recognized another lineage. I felt I was finding the lost poems of John Hoffman, "Who disappeared into the volcanoes of Mexico leaving behind nothing but the shadow of dungarees and the lava and ash of poetry…." as Allen Ginsberg writes in *Howl*. Hoffman was the close friend of Philip Lamantia, and if there's an immediate, American, lineage link for Hamill's surrealism it might begin and end here, with Hoffman/Lamantia. At the Six Gallery Reading, the one where Ginsberg read *Howl* for the first time, the one where Kerouac shouted "Go! Go! Go!" while Cassidy handed round the jug of wine as recorded in *Dharma Bums*, Lamantia read John Hoffman's poems, the few surviving works of his friend, now presumed dead. Here's Hamill in a direct address—

> oh Mexico
> how you betrayed me
> I hurl a glass into the side
> of your sun-splashed murals of democracy
> decaying visions
> of inebriated seers
> Serape of Quetzalcoatl….
>   —from *Troublante*

So the question emerges: How does young Janet Hamill, recently graduated from Glassboro State, South Jersey, conjure up Mexico and the diction of a turn-of-the-century surrealist? "You wrapped around me with the warmth of a cobalt dragon." Questions like this mean nothing here, because, well, we are already in it, our voyage begins as soon as we dip into Hamill's transportive verse. In another poem in *Troublante*, Hamill addresses Vladimir Mayakovsky. The poem is "The Tragedy of Janet Hamill," a direct purloin, with name change, from Mayakovsky's first play—

> O Vladimir
> it's all still
> a stinking mess
> sixty years later
> I'm so
> Hungry
>
> come
> we'll have a chat
> I'll be devoured by your words
> shameless enough I am
> to soak like a bone
> in your alphabet soup

Other poems in the chapbook address Hart Crane—a major mentor, "America's greatest symbolist."

After *Troublante*, Hamill set off on a year-long voyage herself, fulfilling her own visionary poetry. Africa—Sudan and Ethiopia, Egypt, Kenya, Tanzania. And Europe—Spain, France, Italy, what was then Yugoslavia, Greece, Denmark, England. It's as if her poetry willed her trip to happen. There have been subsequent travels but nothing of this scope. Her youthful world journey remains the only major traveling she would do in her life thus far, and her experiences on this road trip will provide the settings for poems the rest of her life, moving from experience to memory and dream to poems, to be joined by other locales as the poems and stories take on their own lives, their own dreams. *The Temple* is set primarily in Morocco and East Africa—

Tangiers and its streets run red
into a labyrinth
the opiate siestas of the afternoon
waltzes of the morphine addicts
on the second floor…

downstairs
the halls fill up with the smoke of anemic rock stars
the glamorous debris of exile
carpets the floor of the lobby
if this is travel
I'd rather ransack with a reverie of dreams
and not the wings in the room drifting in
on a sand cloud of Nembutal

our heads full of dizzy white flowers
and just enough francs for a glass of mint tea

the wind comes around on the tail of a scorpion
night starts to dance in the wands of the Muslims
and something is missing
like magic in love

in the Hotel of Infinite Space

I'll draw my bath and call it sleep
        —from "The Big Sleep"

…

In her second book, *The Temple*, she manages to find Caravaggio in Oaxaca. It's 1980, her first book-length publication, and yet her arcana is already set, her voice already a fully realized hypnotic—

THE TEMPLE
At first there was nothing
and then there was noise
but at first there was nothing
but the sound of the sea
and the sight of birds
gathering in large groups before me
the sun was taking its time
entering the water
like a woman
slow to give birth
the birds were gathering like buzzards
and I was tired of being alone
and falling faint to the illusion
of people trying to approach me
with their metal detectors
I couldn't begin to think of the love
locked in a motel room behind me
the birds were gathering like pterodactyls
and I was tired of being alone

Thus concludes the opening lines of the *The Temple*'s title poem, which ends:

I picked up a stone
and started walking
back to the motel

Who waits there, amidst the metal detectors and pterodactyls? Burroughs,

Bowles, Kerouac, the whole beat cotillion, surrealists, other historic personages—these are Hamill's cohorts in her writings. They put in appearances in her poems, often directly addressed. They give her peace and rest and urgency and poetry itself. Reading her work, you think that these are not mentors, but peers. Friends. Lovers.

Hamill continues to develop her own, open, incantatory style. What to make of the formal cutups, the chant-like repetition,s the sentences that end with periods but do not start with capital letters, the strange blank spaces that begin to appear, divvying up a line? It's as if *speech is overtaking writing*. You are *compelled to run on*. Speech leaves *text in the dust*. But they are here, these printed words. Dust them off and they become the poems in her books. Read,

> The night was coming. I could feel it
> the cold wet dampness and the rain. seeping through the walls
> we took a walk. outside the village. the night was coming
> the cold wet dampness. with the rain illuminating his hair
> Fasil took my hand and led me down into the tombs
> —from "Ethiopie"

> a layer of platinum. morphine
> erotic. waves of criminal water. the painless. pleasure
> of death
> —from "Sacrifice"

A fever dream, an incantation, the thin line separating the living and dead. *The Temple* urgently unfurls, as if the world is being created in lines of poetry, every poem a genesis for some other place, unfettered, image after image taking you further and further from your life, but into a universe no less real—

> On a hot summer night in the city
> I walked through the skies for knifing of stars
> like a panther

perceiving a foreplay of switchblades before me
fighting a battle
inside the arms of a sheltering genie
with pockets of blues and dice
taken from the tusks of an elephant
dying on the plains of Africa
—the opening of "St. Adrian's"

Hamill's third book, *Nostalgia of the Infinite,* a unique dive into ekphrasis, draws its title from a De Chirico painting, titled by Breton. It might just as well have come from Frank O'Hara's "Personism: A Manifesto," his incomparable manifesto/satire of Olson's "Projective Verse." Here O'Hara compares "the nostalgia *of* the infinite" and "the nostalgia *for* the infinite," stating that "nostalgia *of* the infinite represent[s] the greater degree of abstraction, removal, and negative capability (as in Keats and Mallarmé)." And so, to Keats! "Negative Capability... is when Man is capable of being in uncertainties, mysteries, doubts, without any irritable reaching after facts and reason." O'Hara and Keats, who better to attempt to define the capacious noire, the haunting performative of Hamill's poetry?

Poe exploded into a thousand pieces
the abominable atrocities of his mind
scattered and swallowed
by vengeful birds
the angel hooked. the falcon hooded
his bones rattling the quiet of small coast towns
in a whirlpool
the rocks of ages split
                              …
the crows fly out of his skull
—from "The Departure of the Poet (La Mort Extraordinaire)"

Fly me to the moon   Guillaume   propel us
to the end of the world   we'll drink a toast
with history trailing behind   on the fringes
of your white silk aviator scarf

......

Guillaume   this is where I leave you
I'm going to parachute off the wing

Good luck soon   you'll be on the reviewing stand
presiding over celebrations   for a new millennium
      —from "Portrait of Guillaume Apollinaire"

Hamill switches to prose poems and short fictions in her third book, *Lost Ceilings*, which has a Lamantia epigraph, *For a long time I saw no other sky than the ceiling of this room/where, from a chink of plaster, hung the image of paradise...*. somewhere between Poe and flash fiction, between Lydia Davis and science fiction. She also returns to New York City, to the Bleecker Street Cinema, to bookstores and cafés. The "Nocturne" says Leroy Street, but it feels 18th century London, 19th century Paris. The tone is still Africa, Mexico, dreamlike everyday life. But Baudelaire is here, *Avalanche, entomb me in your fall!*, and Fellini, *An Italian ocean liner, like an anchored chandelier, beams its candles across black ripples.*

Before the film runs out her mind will implode. In the Milky Way. She will chart the course of her ship. Burning its history. Time buried. The pulverized relics of the past scattered like ashes. Through lenses in the abyss, she'll gaze at imperishables. Forever.
      —from "Worlds of Time"

Wanting something. Nothing. Absence. Whiteness. Wanting a great annihilation of snows. Wanting something so beautiful as to close the office of the night. A dirge to play on the jukebox of the dispossessed.

At the end of the bar, snow is falling. In the windows on Spring Street, a black and white film of heavenly hosts falling. In slow motion, detached portions of the Milky Way have been falling for hours.
—from "Melancholy Language"

Across the blue, jewel-encrusted masts of the city, voices echo voices with the same assaulting plea. *Take me. Guide me. Illuminate me.* Holy night. *Take me as I am.*

There at their beginning. At the end of Leroy Street, a boy in a blue shirt gathered from the distances between the stars, lends his shoulder to a girl on fire. In an aureole of lamplight. Grace. Beauty of form.
—from "Nocturnes"

Of all that's gone, I keep the cold winter rain against the windows, an anthology of French Symbolist poetry, a corduroy jacket, the proper positioning of the wrist while holding a cigarette and laughter, always laughter.
—from "Rain"

Again, let's try to set a scene. Our poet has had some great jobs, Cinemabilia and the Strand, but her closest friends started to leave the City. And then it is the City itself that starts to change, losing its fluidity and ease, along with its gritty reality and shadows of mystery. A tragic love with a mad poet who took his madness to the street and then—beyond. She moved upstate to a simpler life, with a solid partner, let her writing and painting dictate the movements of her solar system as she found work as a tutor and finally as a librarian, a perfect site for her meditative existence. And then—here comes rock'n'roll.

Here comes rock'n'roll. 1995. A Patti Smith concert at Summer Stage in Central Park, a few thousand in the audience. Patti asks Janet if she will open for her band—a friend opening for a friend, aka a poet opening for a rock goddess. I'll let bass player, Bob Torsello, narrate the meeting, straight out of one of Janet's poems—

"In 1995 Jay LoRobbio and I of the band Shrubs, ventured from 'just upstate' to Central Park Summer Stage to see a Patti Smith performance. The opening act was the poet Janet Hamill. I loved Patti, but I was blown away by Janet's performance. She carried the essence of the band but only had her voice to convey it with. The next day I dropped in on my favorite local bookstore (aka the Goshen (NY) Public Library to see if they had anything by my new favorite poet. This is when it happened—the woman said, that's her, right over there! That's Janet Hamill. Well, she seemed more shocked than happy, but we did chat, and I pitched the idea of a band to accompany her performance. I guess you could say she was 'very reluctant.' Then, in 1997, she heard a John Trudell and Bad Dog CD along with the *Kicks, Joy, Darkness* Kerouac compilation, and she agreed to try it out. The seeds of Janet and Moving Star were sown as Janet read her poems and Jay and I worked out simple arrangements based on what we heard and felt. We eventually added drums and keyboards and performed to enthusiastic crowds. Our debut was at St. Mark's Church in NYC in December of 1997. Janet Hamill and Moving Star recorded 2 CDs: *Flying Nowhere* (2000) and *Genie of the Alphabet* (2005)."

  Lightning striking fluorescent serpents
  This wave of hot breath over my spine

  Let's have another drink
  while the hailstones and demon rain
  bounce off the corrugated roadhouse roof

  Let's swallow our spirits
  and obliterate the night

    *

Moving star bird of fire
open your wings
across the sky
            —the opening of "Moving Star"

How extraordinary for the poet's freeform, unrhymed, celestial lyrics to find a setting in these Jersey boys' (well, Orange County, New York) no-frills garage rock. And in *Body of Water*, a book with a Patti Smith cover and Patti's photos inside, (published by Bowery Books, disclaimer) you start to see some poems which just might serve as rock lyrics. Hint: Why not download Moving Star's two albums, *Flying Nowhere* and *Genie of the Alphabet*, and let your ears hear what your eyes read?

Buster Keaton appears in *Body of Water* with his own poem, "He picked [the royal blue butterfly umbrella] up and walked towards the open windows/a wind caught under the flaps of his pockets/and lifted him off the floor into a series of somersaults." Here you will find "Byron's Time Sheet," *"He's clocked/fourteen hours on his time sheet for one entire year!/but he'll never get paid for it. No. He'll never get paid!"* Fellini returns, too, "I, Fellini/in my forty-third year of beautiful confusion/have been hired/to shoot a masterpiece and I will/riddle the Sistine ceiling with buckshot." And we get the greatest ode to "K E R O U A C" ever written, which the band Lost Ceilings also covered to acclaim—

I had nothing   but I had a grey tee shirt
and I ironed on black velvet letters
K   E   R   O   U   A   C
I had nothing   I had four walls on St. Marks Place
 a bottle of Calvados   and the silence of the universe
 I had nothing   but I had you
—from "K   E   R   O   U   A   C"

Get out your telescopes and naked eyes
we're going to stay out all night long

in the backyards in the campgrounds
what good is heaven for
what good is heaven for
what good is heaven for
if you don't look at the sky
look at the sky
look at the sky
look at the sky
      —from "Star Party"

Gently, lifeless. The pendant boughs of willow
couldn't bear the weight of her. Holding columbines
and cornflowers. Rosemary and rue.
      —from "Tomb for Ophelia"

Hamill's two most recent books, *Knock* and *Real Fire*, play with forms. *Knock* is a travel book that visits six locales—Hollywood, Tijuana, the Atlantic, Giza, San Tropez, and New York. At each stop, we are treated to twelve pantoums, the Malay form that has a complex grid of line repetition which reproduces a dream-like, coming and going texture. Which is appropriate for Hamill in general and these poems in particular, poems born in dreams, recorded first in her dream journal. Each line is divided by spacing into two or three nuggets, which slows the movement, emphasizing the walking/breathing pace.

Within each line, though, the spaces she places stop the poem, allowing each beat to penetrate, hold, then move on. For me, it's a new form, building her performance style into the text—mesmerizing, beguiling, gestural, as close to ritual as a poem text can be. The Azmiri poets in Addis will drink their honey wine, the Yaquí shamans will eat their peyote, and New York will hallucinate poetry, but no one but Hamill will *Knock*.

Real Fire, the most recent book in this collection, is a collaboration of her poems with full color photographs of, you guessed it, real fire, by Richard Baron. Each flame is cast in golds, yellows, and whites against a solid black void; each piece of

Hamill's is written in a completely different form—a litany, "Real Fire," opens the book; there's an Apollinaire-like calligraph in the middle, "Flame"; a piece of prose, "Fire Worshippers (*As told to Viola Cooper, Professor, Oriental Studies, London University, at the Parsee Temple, Madras, India, 1937*)" plays with historicity. The last poem uses the spacing device she created in *Knock*, but while it has repetitions, they are freer, not a pantoum. It's a sweet, slant collaboration.

So here, in your hands, *A Map of the Heavens*. The title of the Selected Poems, actually a prose meditation with 1,971 stars, puts in an appearance from the collection *Lost Ceilings*. It concludes with the poet sitting at her desk atop a pyramid, her suitors, approaching, step by step (a Mayan pyramid, I'd imagine). She of course is writing the piece we are reading, which is a map, a map to places humans have never been. But, of course, we have been there; she has taken us there. We travel the globe, and then we leave the globe and travel there. She is our Baudelaire. Here are poems from seven books written over 42 years. Someday a hologram of Janet Hamill will pop up and read them to you, trance you. Until then, you're on your own. Just trust your poet guide, and yourself, and the poems will lead you to places you could never imagine, but now hold in the palm of your hand.

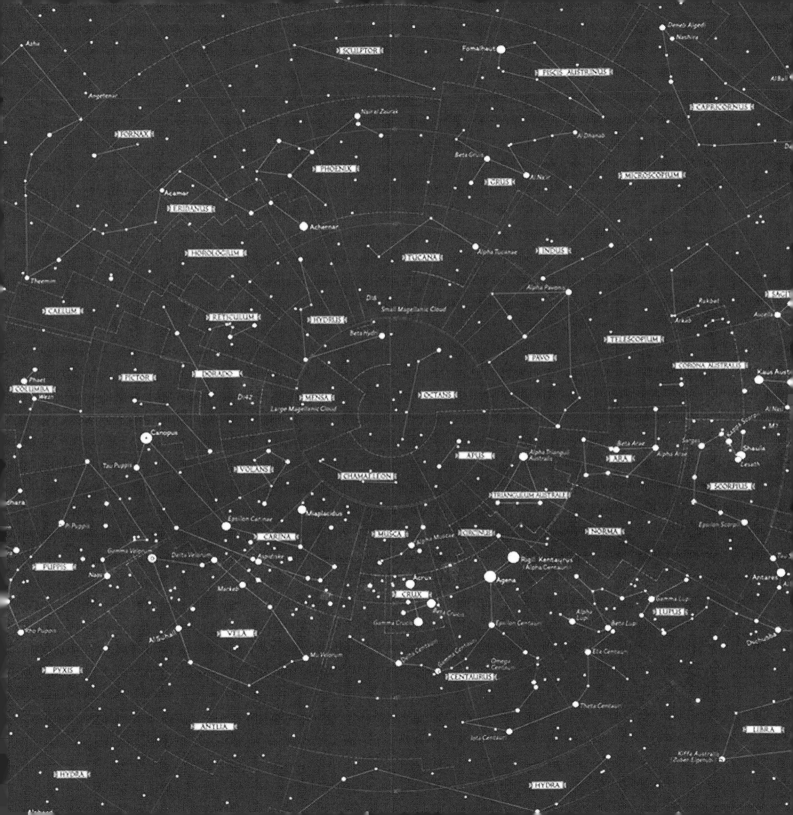

…All that has dark sounds has duende…Those dark sounds are the mystery…
The duende needs the trembling of the moment and then a long silence….

Federico Garcia Lorca

from *TROUBLANTE*
(1975)

…something to worry about,
to be disturbed, troubled by….
The troublante, the difficulty.
Lord, I forget what language I'm speaking.

Carlos Fuentes

TROUBLANTE. The cold objective eyes
set in their tray like ice cubes
Striking in jungle towns. The Yucatan
The small brown priests with their agonizing science of time
The orbits of Venus whirling around.
A pressure chamber in the air
The facial skin torn out and pulled
The foreheads pointed like ugly birds
like exaggerated warps of flesh as you say it. Troublante
Your flesh forever peaches and cream on an Easter sundae
I kiss and walk away with a mouth full of whip cream
But your throat. Troublante. Making the sound of a hornbill
Congested it is. Bottle-necked. A backed-up pipe
Your throat clogged with an obstruction of black orchids
The hot southern breeze obstructed
The pounding heart in your groin

The puffy Anglo face. The apple cheeks packed with ice
A trickle from your eyes. Those icebergs. Troublante
you know this is where it begins
The writing
the view from the top of Palenque
the fields of golden boys
drunken kisses of the sun
erotic rhythms of his tail hung down

Would you dare to rape them with a lashing tongue
dive down like a vulture on the ball courts
without convulsions or the lining of your stomach ripping?

BELLADONNA

who is it wants me
who makes the animal noise
who walks barefoot
while I'm sleepless
those bare feet
so small and delicate
that stick to the linoleum
while all the while
death's making noise
like wings flapping

Belladonna

I'm helpless
my hands are tied before you
the raven tonight

black wingspread
the devil's airplane
come land on me

raven crashing
raven tearing
Belladonna
more than life-size
you
like an angel of Poe
you
like his hallucinated pilot
but you
the devil tonight
what makes you want me

Belladonna

sending sounds
that come and go
a lady laughing
a lady moaning
a lady naked in her bathrobe
do you want me
to want her

Belladonna

Belladonna

raven more than life-size
raven the devil tonight
if you want me
come and eat me
eat me
come and eat me

THE LONESOME DEATH OF H. CRANE

the dawn was revealing his chest
like a land-locked sailor
over the ruins
of the pyramid of the sun

I wished he'd rain
like a heaven of alcohol
into my face
tightening like the skin on a drum
in a mirror over the bar
dissolving into a round of lacerating
light cut like a splinter of shot glass
into my heart's
muscle of thirst
spleen for a flask of tequila

Eagle of Mesquil

your nights were a hell of cantinas
searching the soul of a serpent
coiling the ground of the dawn
like a prostitute
spilling the earth with a urine
of cigarette butts and beer
under a table
baptizing my face
with a shower
of pristiline star-shattered nerves

oh Mexico
how you betrayed me
I hurl a glass into the side
of your sun-splashed murals of democracy
decaying visions
of inebriated seers

serape of Quetzalcoatl

you wrapped around me with the warmth of a cobalt dragon
on days rising like predatory mist
over jungles full of copulating birds
my mind racing
like a thoroughbred horse's head in flames
through a field of discarded bottles
the apocalyptic jockey
winking an eye at the sun

*

and now
let the ship swing further
into the gulf stream's
warm waters of Caribbean lush

The days of the roaring boy are done
I'm ready for death
like a patient in my pajamas
to dive like a dolphin into the sea
breaking light
like a splinter of shot glass
into the mouth
of a hungry white shark
and let them comb the sea like scavengers
for the bones of my land-locked wings

THE TRAGEDY OF JANET HAMILL

Vladimir
O Vladimir
it's all still
a stinking mess
sixty years later
I'm so
Hungry

what would fill me
nothing less than a leap at you
into heaven
springing off a diving board
like Kamensky's plane

roger –
over and out

come
we'll have a chat
I'll be devoured by your words
shameless enough I am
to soak like a bone
in your alphabet soup

O Vladimir
my hole's so big
and all remains
a stinking mess
like Futurism –
Ha!
I could declare it myself
with a kick in the pants

you swam in them –
the winds of change
and now
what's left
what's fixed
nothing
remains
but restlessness

I know
had I known you
I'd have loved you
had I money
I'd have fixed your teeth
selfishly
to run my tongue along the keys
the portal to your heart

O bashful precursor –
I want to make it bare
undisciplined lightning strike
but Vladimir
the restlessness
enormous
hole that it is
still
so
Hungry!

RESIDENCIA EN LA TIERRA

microcosm. macrocosm.
star. quasar. steady state
the iguana expanding through time
walking out of the sea
onto the continent of South America
in the third year. inhaling the air
the humid seeping of time in the tropics

steady state. through the years. the unraveling ball
the constant inhaling of air. all the stored-up knowledge
in the lung cells of the first reptile. low flame
the sun's intoxicating. time is a delicate drug in Ecuador

lazy. lack of movement. sunspots.
every other century a vessel bursting
debris. cracks. faults in the land.
Peru is wracked with earthquakes
restless shifting. the great bang explosion
of the Andes overnight. catastrophic

a mere split on the side of iguana
a jolt to his grip. his gears
his procession over the continent
pulling his belly along the ground
he wants to make love
but they eat him like chicken. split him in two
matter reduces to matter

the rains are strange in the Amazon. river of reptiles

CARTE BLANCHE

I feel the need to expose myself
to an alien world

to drink of innocence in a burning landscape

and pursue the tastes of different men
so thereby make them one

the triple child of heaven and hell
　　　　and the middle kingdom

the heroine: daughter of Eve

from *THE TEMPLE*
(1980)

Take me to the other end of the city
where no one knows the difference between you and me.

Paul Bowles

THE BIG SLEEP

In the Hotel of Infinite Space
flies buzz around like dreams of disease
the neurotic little specs jump out of the eyes
like armies after something to eat

an afternoon light of solar orange from Spain
infested with blood

Tangiers and its streets run red
into a labyrinth

the opiate siestas of the afternoon
waltzes of the morphine addicts
on the second floor
your soothing voice
to offer tea
in spite of wild philosophies
outside the window
in arousing combat
like dragon winds coming in from the sea
inciting fires
on the street of the somnambulists

downstairs
the halls fill up with the smoke of anemic rock stars
the glamorous debris of exile
carpets the floor of the lobby

if this is travel
I'd rather ransack with a reverie of dreams
and not the wings in the room drifting in
on a sand cloud of Nembutal

you turn your back into a sleep
that goes for hours without dreams
sedated
baby
how long will we last
like a séance

the smoke curls out of my painted wooden pipe
inhaling brooding gods and melancholy losses
of a sweet Arab song

my subtle capture by the Berbers
in a tent of religious light
indoctrinated by Fatima into a cult
of erotic evenings
in the harem of a crazy blue-eyed prince

the way I wooed him with my wisdom
and his knowledge of my charms
bestowing gifts in leagues of stallions
for the mounts of my disciples
stampeding trails of unreasoned sacking
dragon strongholds
and purging ungiving hearts

you hold your back in a tension of early Egyptian reliefs

how long will we last like a sleepwalk through time
passing in a novel of bookstores
in the late afternoon on a hill
in the French section of town
our heads full of dizzy white flowers
and just enough francs for a glass of mint tea

the wind comes around on the tail of a scorpion
night starts to dance in the wands of the Muslims
and something is missing
like magic in love

in the Hotel of Infinite Space

I'll draw my bath and call it sleep

SUBTERRANEOUS

The heart thinks constantly. this can't be changed
like a spaceship. placed on automatic. without control
me now. like a shadow entering a valley of dissipated angels
under a storm. of red-shifts and radio haloes
the stars are transmitting. into the mountains
the ceilings of mosques are crumbling
before my eyes. an astrolabe drops
like the intricate face of a wheel of fortune
and tigers and memories. come through the wall with a fist

the battery sits. like my soul gone dead
before desire. the long green fingers of death
creeping up behind my back. somewhere
in the depths of the earth. where the fires of mars are burning
my hair shirt hangs on a rack

ETHIOPIE

Arrived in Aksum around noon and checked into the Queen of Sheba Hotel
I was dying for a cup of coffee. just to get the blood circulating
We'd been riding since 6 A.M. through the cold muddy towns of the mountains
there were monkeys. behind every tree I could see them
running for shelter. from the rain falling on the roof of the bus

In the village. I tried to overlook the sickness and the eyes
caked with an excrement of flies

The market was small and the women sat beneath umbrellas
all the grains were spread out on blankets. saffron. dried red peppers
and salt. Like pools of light in a landscape without any sun
the boys walked closely behind me. wrapped in shrouds. carrying crosses
made out of stone. in their hands. all the mud washed down from the monasteries
I think. I wanted the one around his neck and he offered to give it away as a gift
if I promised to send him a dictionary from Addis Ababa. I assumed
there were bookstores

In the hotel. I felt an urge to repack the luggage
I was ashamed of the equipment and supplies we were procuring
all the jewelry and the baskets. in the sack. I saw a spider
There were voices in the rooms. off the courtyard. laughing
whores and thieves. deported from Sudan

The night was coming. I could feel it
the cold wet dampness and the rain. seeping through the walls
we took a walk. into the village. the night was coming
the cold wet dampness. with the rain illuminating his hair
Fasil took my hand and led me down into the tombs

We were standing on the platform of Aksum. stelae falling all over the grounds
as the moon was receding. He took my hand and led me down into the tombs
with his matches and newspaper torches
the ceiling ignited like so many faces of angels

HOTEL RABAT/SLEEPING FIT

It's the beginning of something/there's
a total white field/above the sheets
of the Hotel of Paris/my life is on trial
for sins I committed/discarded
the jumpsuits/the floor of the closet
is floating in blood/from the knives
in the kitchen sink/as I wash
all the dishes of innocent eyes/burn
in an executioner's hood/in the darkness
a breeze shifts/like a frozen hand
under the sheets/the night crawls/like a lizard
over a glacier/my heart retreats/into
the walls/like a lamb/I lift my shirt
to the Snake of All Possible Dreams
and surrender/to fear/and the thorns
in my spine/in the Temple/at 4 A.M.

SACRIFICE

There's a fire inside the mountain where a puma rests
on the continent of silence. the unfurnished living room
in space. where now a sacrifice takes place. behind
a landmass of skeletons. the ice floes creep. long
lines of leopards in the snow. you have to go. to keep
the logs keep burning in a halestrom. the corpse
of a bat in the night. stills. the windowsills are dirty
and hope trembles on the legs of a dying.   praying mantis
Solstice. leave me now like this. with the sun bleeding
passing Spanish hearts in my hands. the soft white flesh
of a tender neck. thrown back into submission. a face
full of resignation. the eyes pleading. close me now
like this. forever. shut the light. release the seas
the endless ocean voyages of melancholy. ions flare
in the fire. the bookshelves rise. like a tower
of the arcane world. you cling. in a silk cocoon. of a yellow
sheet. like a wing. of Baal's angels. the ancients
press on your skull. like a tumor. the manuscripts curl
in a flame.   and I light a light in the darkness. the cigarettes
drop to the floor. and they reappear. the long lines
of leopards in the snow. it's time to go. into a courtyard
into an unfurnished living room in space. to make
your grace. beneath the jaws of a generous lion
teeth capped down to the bone. a layer of platinum
morphine. erotic. waves of criminal water
the painless. pleasure of death

with a bite to your jugular
you break on through
releasing the final
vials of congenital poison

pints of blood
and millenniums
of endless
ocean
voyages

*

Gone away…gone away…across the wide white sea
you can close your eyes…all the pain is gone…the moonless shores
are towering and steep…frozen reliquaries of sleep…forever
is the mercy of the polar night…no flaming nimbuses…no hell
no crown of petrified thorns…no hope trembling…no knives
ripping through the silk on your back…no wings of Baal's angels
casting shadows before you and behind   no wind…no sacrament
of rain…nothing remains   you can bid your boat away…all the pain
is gone in a rapture of bones flesh…fluids…veins
and dreams of long lines of leopards in the snow

CARAVAGGIO

I'm in a small Mexican town outside
Oaxaca/the sun is crawling like an
orange serpent through the window
a white sail disappears over the jungle
I walk through the rooms in a green
satin slip/amulets on either shoulder
strap/bleeding hearts of Mary/Magdalene
laces in black are wrapped around my ankles
Caravaggio dreams in the bedroom
heat siesta/wandering the waterfronts
of all the ports/in all the cities
of the world/his skin is flushed
with a mild fever/and blue gulf stream
fly fish lie across his thighs/the walls
perspire like the exhausted flesh
of a youthful Bacchus/damp indulgent sheets
a parrot screams behind my back
the scarlet blood drops leave a trail
down my leg/the laces tighten
and I feel so sore inside
a raving barracuda took a bite of something tender

BEAUTIFUL DREAMER

Drunk on rhythms and wine
an orchestration of languages
running eternally
through the arteries of time

the sun is setting
in a big red blotch
in the center of your forehead
forcing love
outside of its temple
and on to the skin
where the dream is drawn
and frantic waves
of electric light
strip the skin of its pigment

I want you to hold me
because the night's
stalking it's young
like an animal
held in captivity
and white angelic wingspreads
seem to protrude from your shoulders
like birds
releasing themselves
from a cage

the ground trembles
your whole body shakes

at the thought of the landscape
evolving into eternity
the horses roam across the plains
and kick up the dust with their hooves
in a graceful innocence

as you bow your head
believing for a moment
that all your bleeding memories
will take leave of your heart
by themselves

ST. ADRIAN'S

On a hot summer night in the city
I walked through the skies for knifing stars
like a panther
perceiving a foreplay of switchblades before me
fighting a battle
inside the arms
of a sheltering genie
with pockets of blues and dice
taken from the tusks of an elephant
dying on the plains of Africa

bones decayed. ivory cells. the thick wrinkled skin
on a vacant-lotted city. crying seconds
over Labor Day headlines of accidents

In the streets
I walked to a lousy bar
where the liquor didn't work
because I was looking for excitement
with a nose full of snow
all in white. like a timeless Moroccan belle
in the casbah. where the fans hang low
from the ceiling
inviting an easy pace to keep you cool

New York—
my endearing
air-conditioned respiratory system

St. Adrian's—
and the walls perspiring
like the lungs of an aging poet
enraptured in nicotine
whirlpools of distracted desire
beneath green suspended pool table lamps

a tiger cried
like a captured girl in my mind
and everyone drank
like a little bit crazy too

THE GREEN SUIT

Now I go about me in my Green Suit
brandishing double-edged letter openers
crested with dragon heads. I slip in and out
of all the irresistible envelopes in the world
postmarked Freedom of Space

In Timbuktu dancing under the constellation of Scorpios
with the chief of his tribe. the sands are rich in mineral mines
of diamonds and lapis. under the earth where the dervishes spin
I slip in and out of all the irresistible envelopes in the world
postmarked Forget the Past

In Paris where the poets wrote poems for a living
the Surreal hotels and motherships circled around the cafés
like open invitations to Tierra Incognito
Tierra del Fuego and Tierra Misterioso
all the pages and pages of unwritten manuscripts
locked inside the closets. the barges and pockets of their suits
the interior landscapes. spread all over their sleeves

The Mountains. The Deserts
and The Faces of Cities to Come

The lovers riding their horses into the sunset
looking straight ahead. knowing they're not alone
in their Green Suits

A CHANGE OF SKIN

American metaphors on Nevada highways in the August sun. billboards
exposing themselves like aroused organs. beneath the deafening
sound of the landscape. trying to keep everything in perspective

we came out here from the cities
we came out here from our heat and frustrations
we came out here to change our skin

in white Chevrolet convertibles. breaking through the barriers
that lie ahead. a thousand and one enclosed shopping malls
crushed like dirt under the wheels of the car
the snakeskin on the side of the road
the cool vegetation
and seclusion in shadows
of Wild Horse Canyon

the snakeskin on the side of the road

we came out here
when the movement of thunder and rain was filling the atmosphere
clouds pressed down on the rooftops
causing cracks in the ceilings
in the hallways
the angel of mercy was turned away
by a lean white boy
pressing his finger to an angry gun
on the dark side of the moon
the Sea of Tranquility
bombarded by a shower of meteorites

the snakeskin on the side of the road

we came out here in the great masochistic night
guided by the fires burning on the mountains

                                    *

Nevada highways…August sun…glaring white teeth
of a toothpaste smile…a hundred miles…into the valley
of paradise…mobile homes…*the snakeskin on the side of the road*
I'm so lonesome I could die…in a dark saloon…in the afternoon
the desert comes up to the door of my heart…blond sandstone
cliffs…basalt buttes…Eureka…Route 80…eighty miles
to Humboldt's Natural History Museum…a million fossils
in the arroyo beds…dinosaur bones…salt flats…silver veins
the Comstock load…there's nothing on the radio but intergalactic
noise…Mars on Earth…a rock with wings…Shoshones…coyotes
in the clumps of sagebrush…sixty miles…fifty miles
the snakeskin on the side of the road…the ghosts of the first men
corpse dust of the lizard king…the west is the best…the sky
the sky…the sky…raven circling overhead…waiting for us to die

THE TEMPLE

At first there was nothing
and then there was noise
but at first there was nothing
but the sound of the sea
and the sight of birds
gathering in large groups before me
the sun was taking its time
entering the water
like a woman
slow to give birth
the birds were gathering like buzzards
and I was tired of being alone
and falling faint to the illusion
of people trying to approach me
with metal detectors
I couldn't begin to think of the love
locked in a motel room behind me
the birds were gathering like pterodactyls
and I was tired of being alone

On the boardwalk
I stopped beneath the paper mâché mask of a woman
laughing hysterically into my eyes
over the marquee of the funhouse
the lights were coming on slowly
like beacons
off the coast of a lunar sea
the last hermetic outposts of the mind

For fifty cents I paid the fee
and walked through corridors
lined with mirrors
feeling like a piece of jelly
clinging to a mold
the long black cape was brushing against the walls
and the halls were empty
when a woman bellowed
from the bowels of the interior —

You think that you know everything
you think you've been around and burned and glorified
and know everything
but just like a dog who thinks he knows when his master
 is going to feed him
sometimes you don't even know that much
sometimes you don't even listen
you don't see a thing
sometimes you're so out in space
that nothing penetrates your senses

And the face of love becomes unrecognizable
outside on the beach
as the night descends
like a hero
trailing his leg across the sand

ii

To the tombs in the Valley of the Kings she said
the cool dark interiors
the walls and ceilings covered with stars
the timelessness
the penetrating timelessness
in the funhouse
where she stood at the end of a tunnel
like a pillar of green fire
releasing properties of magnetism
through her skin
her eyes burning like white hot pokers
at the bottom of a cave
she said….

You think that you know everything….

But I could only remember the Ferris wheel
the lights and the sound of the sea
the motel room
where you lay sleeping
under sheets
the notebooks and ashtrays
the demons and the angels

I turned to go

There are things too vast and incomprehensible to think of….
don't think that you know everything

iii

Then walking ramps
led to revolving barrels
to more walking ramps and distorting mirrors
to the boardwalk
with all the electric anonymity of a crowd at night
the neon at the Arcadia
advertising highlights from *The Chateau of Desire*
fear and pornography
taking hold of my imagination with a leather glove
the gripping sensation of love
ran through my legs
and I wondered how much of it was illusion

Her chiselled emerald face
the people trying to approach me with metal detectors
the birds
your smile
and the desk clerk
aliens from Mars
leaning over the Star Flight Pinball Machine
with a young girl
breathing in the night like an heiress

iv

At first there was nothing
and then there was noise
but at first there was nothing
until your voice broke the silence
like a bullet crashing through a pane of glass

I sat on the beach
the birds rose out of the sea
like tongues
there were conversations between us
that were better left unspoken

I picked up a stone
the horizon was beginning to look the tabula rasa again
and time
and space
and pterodactyls
no longer existed
except as the occupations of an idle mind

I picked up a stone
and started walking back
to the motel

THE POET ASSASSINATED

enregistre et

Reproduction
des 58 images
en reconstitution
de la
petite machine

André Lhermitte

from *NOSTALGIA OF THE INFINITE* (1992)

*To you, intoxicated with enigmas and happy
in the twilight, to you whose souls are led
astray by flutes to labyrinthine abysses….*

Friedrich Nietzsche

*A painter has painted an enormous red chimney
Which a poet worships like a deity.*

Giorgio de Chirico

THE DEPARTURE OF THE ARGONAUTS

Hear me. you who tore at the warm red meat
on the altar of embarkations. you who
witnessed the fire with its smoke-black wings
winding their way towards heaven. you who
drank and danced on the beach
now the dawn breathes life into our canvas
propitious winds crown the sea
with long white manes. and lift the clouds
from the sky. a blue of origins
hear me. you who were told in a dream
to make this voyage. now the time has come
to fix the oars and set sail for unknown waters
leaving the noises of the land far behind

THE DEPARTURE OF THE POET
(La Mort Extraordinaire)

Poe exploded into a thousand pieces
the abominable atrocities of his mind
scattered and swallowed
by vengeful birds
the angel hooked. the falcon hooded
his bones rattling the quiet of small coast towns
in a whirlpool
the rocks of ages split

to dig down
and reverse the velocity
chemicals spin in a centrifuge
call stop
and the lid is hurled into space

bone china
luminescence
smooth white skin of an innocent
embalmed and rest in peace
the crows fly out of his skull

Metaphysical Interior

Waters flow on. beyond this room. filling and emptying
the moon in a white funereal mask.   bending down
over the bare ground. littered with wing feathers. horns
and animal pelts

A dark star falls. a leaf unfolds. is green. turns yellow
and withers away with the wind

Beyond this room.   with painted leaves on the ceiling
this room with a bed of clouds. this room with obsidian mirrors
and a tabernacle on a marble table. this ancient heart
of a room. impervious to the tyranny of inconstancy
this room with a bridegroom and a bride
undressing themselves. forever

MORNING MEDITATION

A.

Still summer morning
with a god's golden eye
rising out of the sea
silk undulating curtains
over the window
I awake. refreshed
the taste of sleep
in my mouth
salt spraying my tongue
in the dark green harbor
where dolphins
swam through the night
like wet petals
of moonlight

B.

Abandoned by the night
the knives of violent sun
stab at my eyes
split open. like wounds
on a windowsill
a pair of bloody pomegranates
all is dizzy
swollen. nauseous
fluttering in tatters
the curtain's
torn aside
and wild-eyed music
from the mountains
rings in my ears

THE MYSTERY AND MELANCHOLY OF A STREET

In the midst of the empty city
lies the street of chance
in the midst of all the dark and twisted sailors
tearing out the linings of their mattresses
a vast and virgin avenue unfolds

Before a painted backdrop
a burning building
and a pink tower of insomnia

A vast and virgin avenue unfolds

For the anxious mariners
with an echo in their hearts
conceived in the bellies of their mothers —
the naked ladies
wearing diamond tiaras in the vestibules —
visited night after night
by gentleman callers
with fast platinum thought bullets
hungry voices and flowers

THE SEER/THE SPHINX AT SEA

Seen from a distance. your bare
shoulders under the lamplight
nocturnal. moon-dusted mountains
of snow. sequestered. in eternity
behind your eyes. the wind blows
over the sea. stirring the surface
of the water. as you board your
gold seraphic boat. with thoughts
beginning and beginning again

recumbent. rock-carved. reading
pages of Greek philosophy
the small pine island of the gods appears
a raw and brilliant emerald in its matrix

so crowned. the sea takes you away
in her blue-gloved arms she takes you
far from the keening choruses
on the beach. beating time on harps and drums
while the rain drives in their faces

Portrait Of Guillaume Apollinaire

Fly me to the moon   Guillaume   propel us
to the end of the world   we'll drink a toast
with history trailing behind   on the fringes
of your white   silk   aviator scarf

Guillaume   keep your eyes on the clouds
or are they horses   while I attend
to the uncorking of the Moët et Chandon

To the Twentieth Century   your baby   Guillaume

What a splash you made   driving up the Blvd. Montparnasse
in your little car   and stopping in front of La Couple
My good people   you said   to the crowd
dancing on the sidewalk   step aside
I personally will deliver this century

Always with a poem in your pocket
a big belly laugh   in your hands
carved African fetishes from Dahomey
hot stuff
the thieves of Paris
the painters of Paris
the whores of Paris
the poets of Paris
the street musicians of Paris
sitting down at your table
like courtiers to a king

Guillaume   those were the days

The genii of the future appeared
in the pale blue smoke of your Russian cigarettes
l'esprit nouveau   and invention
were your *cris de coeur*
until the wee hours   the café cat
slept at your feet
and you were Orpheus   in infinite space

Galaxies beyond galaxies
pornography palmistry Simultanism
streetcars   locomotives   cinema
Cubism   detective stories   Jesus Christ
and   Hermes Trismegistus
sorcery   Surrealism   cartography
alchemy   astrology   speed   change   architecture
and love potions of the ancient Aztecs
anything   and everything
tied into a *bouquet garni* to flavor the pot

And when the last carafe was empty
and everyone was gone
the pretty redhead leaving
on someone else's arm
you traced the chronic spirals of your melancholy on a napkin

Unaware
that if the Phoenix dies one evening
morning sees it born anew

A new day
new fires in the hair of the women you would meet
along the quays   new books in the stalls
the glare of a new century
and in your sunglasses   the twin reflected images
of the Eiffel Tower

Look   Guillaume   they are horses
horses in the sky   on your left   the Milky Way
blows out the window
of the universe   a billion stars
threaded on a curtain of heirloom lace

Some more champagne

Guillaume   at this altitude   I can see you
sitting in the trenches   on the Western Front
with a copy of the *Mercure de France*
suddenly   there's a big explosion
and your blood streams down over the pages
bull's eye
a fragment of enemy shell
has struck you in the temple

In your prime   Guillaume

Having worn a bandage of glory   around your head
Having known long months of convalescence
having married your nurse
having been bombarded with flowers
at a banquet in your honor
having still so many things to say
you stretched out on your bed
with your helmet at your side

and succumbed   to Spanish influenza

Seventy years ago   Guillaume

and since then   you've been serving time   for soaring
too close to the sun   you've been flying around
in this ancient craft   watching the Twentieth Century
wind down   while your hair turned white

But now   that old Phoenix music is hovering overhead
for your ascension

On to the city made of emeralds and solid gold
over a sea of glass   through the roof of the world
flying in formation   with angels on horseback
to the gates of heaven   parting

Guillaume   this is where I leave you
I'm going to parachute off the wing

Good luck   soon you'll be on the reviewing stand
presiding over celebrations
for a new millennium

Adieu   adieu   until we meet again

FÊTE DAY

A musician traveling in a hot dry country came upon a procession in a small village. Dancing through the dusty streets were men, women and children in robes of orange and purple silk, with yellow powder on their faces. In the middle of the parade, borne aloft on a litter covered with flowers, were the bronze statues of two lions. It was the day of the annual Feast of the Temple Guardians.

At noon the celebrants entered the temple and closed the heavy wooden doors behind them, leaving the musician to wander the deserted streets. Overwhelmed by sunlight after a few moment's meandering, he stepped into a shaded courtyard. Fountain-stirred water tumbled from terrace to terrace into pools arranged geometrically among fruit trees. In an unlocked room facing the garden, he found a piano and notebooks filled with music paper. And in this cool, marble-walled room, to the accompaniment of birds outside a grilled window, he sat down and composed for the first time in years. Hours of effortless composition were followed by the sound of explosions coming from the street. With his trance thusly interrupted, the musician paused to take stock of what he had written — one long symphonic work, which he'd titled at the outset *The Song of God.*

Carrying his achievement in the many notebooks under his arm, he stepped out into the street. Night had fallen, the streets had been watered down and children, with faint traces of yellow powder on their faces, were throwing firecrackers against the sides of the houses.

THE RED TOWER

In a sea I lived. in solitude. and it bore me up
on a wave. over the marketplace. pacing
like an injured animal. it bore me up
over the land of sleep and poison flies
a tower rising through the clouds of maleficence
my tongue. in flames. my fountain. overflowing
in the cold night air. while strong winds blew
along the battlements

naked stars. millions and millions of miles away
on the open heights. I could feel their light
entering my skin

above the din of buzzing flies. I rose
above the parasites and bloodsuckers
who drained me of my will
swallowing fire. I climbed up to my wilderness
with a flight of frozen songbirds
in my heart

THE SONG OF LOVE

Magnificent angel. in your white convulsive arms
I'm a small green bird of song
singing in praise of her cage. my ankles
lend themselves willingly to your bracelets

I'm a succulent pink dessert. the edible fruit
of a jungle flower. begging to be eaten
in your white convulsive arms
magnificent angel. I'm a dancing flame

Clinging to your eyes of blue mirrored glass
my desire renews itself endlessly
in waves breaking over my anchored waist
waves that smell of fish and sweat

The intimate odors of a summer night
wrap around me. in your white convulsive arms
magnificent angel. I'm lifted up with moonlight
bleaching my skin. to the measureless ocean overhead.

NOSTALGIA OF THE INFINITE

The sunbaked roads are banked with fires
rising to a sky of grey and yellow gases
acid pools breed mosquitoes. laying eggs
on hot motionless days

This place embalms me
so far away from home

A stale breeze blows. the flow of time
into seasons has been disrupted. Here
the rivers boil and evaporate continually
and all things are benumbed

Only the night is hospitable
extending its long white hand
only the cold restorative night —
infinite clusters of pulverized starlight
fathoms gleaming in their eyes. a phalanx
of leopards strides across the empyrean heading for home

There is no end. no bottom. no ceiling to the night

Dancing without adornment. pores open
like doors on the edge of a splendid sea
where dark blue waves converge
in grateful anonymity

*

Bloodred

The sun crawls into a chasm of the afternoon
how deep. how inescapable this landgrave
of chiseled teeth. tongues swollen
and covered with foam. not even dogs
will drink the water in the wells here

*

Hasten the night. and its curative fingers
drawing the tension out of the earth

Inviolate darkness falls. a thousand sleepless birds
spread their wings throughout the night
brushing each other gently. until they're less than dust
drifting towards a farther plane

to be invisible. to reach the highest tower
this is the endowment of the night

Bathing in verdant surrender. limbs lifted
from lassitude are buoyed by the wide silk
sails of the night. arching and bending
with each wave. upon wave. upon wave

THE ENIGMA OF A DAY

Here and there a lizard runs in fright on a wall
splitting apart. the earthquake lays its long and trembling
siege of the city. under green skies

A yellow angel flies. from roof to roof. waiting
for the shadow of the equestrian to fall. across the square

The sun is passing from the center of its arch
the last train has left the station

Orange toads adhere to windows. White ghost-ship sails billow
throughout the city the sound of falling stones
is heard as the mountains move

A somnambulist meditating on his reflection
in the still mirror of a fountain. is flocked around
by innumerable birds. while at his feet
his faithful lion sits. unwilling to leave him out of love

THE MELANCHOLY OF DEPATURE
(La Messagère Nocturne)

Standing on the promenade
on the last night at sea
I can see the signal fires
along the coast of Morocco —
a welcoming committee
of flickering electric lights
strung from Essaouira to Agadir

Down in the lowest deck
the Yugoslavian crew
is throwing a party for everyone
with plenty of vodka
Polish beer
And rock n' roll

My soul
adoring the sea
would like to plunge
into its sadness

So immense
and inconsolable
by the phosphorescence
glowing in the wake of the ship

Tomorrow in Casablanca
I'll set my feet down
on a brand-new continent of shop windows
filled with silver jewelry
shining like fresh minted currency

But tonight
holding a shell to my ear
I hear your irrepressible voice
calling from across the Atlantic

Don't forget me.
Please don't forget me.

I'm posting these words
With a white pigeon
Hoping he'll navigate the distance
that lies between us
by the stars

AUTUMN MELANCHOLY

Catherine de Montchensi was a young Occitanian wife in the age of *l'amour courtois* and the jeweled sunburst on the Virgin's breast. The age of hell's bedlam—*janua diaboli*—the earthly woman awakened to her nature. She had been betrothed in childhood to an older man—a marriage arranged by her father in the interests of land—and at the age of thirteen, she left her home in Pau to enter her husband's castle in Toulouse. Animated by a high spirit, Catherine quickly mastered the courtly conventions—hawking, playing chess, learning letters, singing, and playing musical instruments. But in spite of these amusements, her time passed melancholically. For although her husband provided her with every luxury, she resented her conjugal subjection, and longed for a love that was freely sought and freely given.

One day as she was training her goshawk by the river Catherine encountered Arnaut Vidal, engaged in the composition of a chanson. So strong was her attraction for the troubadour, that she released her hawk, letting it fly from her wrist. And the jongleur, feeling the same magnetic pull, dropped his rebec in mid-song. That afternoon they began an idyll, fearlessly following their heart's urges, making love in a grotto beyond the castle's walls. After three months of clandestine meetings, Catherine's husband interrupted the romance. He had grown suspicious of his young wife and followed her into the fields. Enraged by his cuckolding, he reacted violently. Catherine was brought back to the castle, where she was fitted with an iron girdle of chastity. And the lord's hired men chased Arnaut to the edge of the fiefdom, where he was brutally castrated. The tragedy led Catherine to take up a veil of sorrow in a convent, while Arnaut found a refuge in monasticism.

Five hundred years after the forceful separation, the remains of Catherine de Montchensi were discovered beneath the abbey in St. Guillem-Le Deserte, along with a box containing chansons by Arnaut Vidal. The exquisite lyrics praised the young wife for her beauty and refinement. They spoke of the ennobling quality of love and described woman as the ladder on which to climb to heaven. As soon as the bones were found they were brought to the square in Pau where a monument, which still stands today as white as a Pyrenean snowdrift, was erected—a beautiful female figure enveloped in loose drapery, reclining on a sarcophagus. The face of the figure wears a melancholic expression and the body's posture suggests a convalescent, eternally recovering from a sickness of the heart. Throughout the centuries, the statue was perceived by its beholders to be a saint of love. People brought flowers and placed them at its base. There they knelt and prayed for an intercession in their love lives.

Two hundred years after Catherine de Montchensi's remains were discovered, the bones of Arnaut Vidal were unearthed beneath the monastery in Limoges, along with a box containing letters from Catherine. The letters reminded the troubadour of how much like an altar was the bed of consummation with his lady, and they compared the nourishment of the spiritual fire of erotic love to the nourishment that the lover of God received from the bread and wine of the Eucharist. As soon as Arnaut's remains were found, they were brought to Pau and laid beside Catherine in a marble sarcophagus, beneath the effigy of a magnificent reclining naked youth, with a face that wore an archaic smile. On the day of its unveiling, a great ceremony was held in the square. Dignitaries came from as far away as Paris. An orchestra played the overture to Wagner's *Tristan und Isolde*. As the music reached its rapturous peak, the canvas cloth covering the statue was removed, revealing the lovers, side by side, with the inscription *conjugium in aeternum* chiseled into the stone of their common plinth.

On the day following the ceremony, the strange events began. The first thing noticed was the altered expression on Catherine's face. Gone was her melancholic expression. It had been replaced with an archaic smile. And the folds of drapery covering her body had disappeared. Even more startling was the sudden, powerful pull one felt on approaching the statues. It was as though they were imbued with magnetism. Many were frightened by the changes. But many more realized that a miracle had occurred; and within days of the coming together of the young wife and the troubadour, a cult of love was initiated.

People in love, and people seeking love, came to the square with flowers. They stood at the base of the monuments, where the aura was so intense that one became endowed with the virtues of the lovers on the sarcophagi. Worshippers held candlelight vigils and slept at the feet of the statues, hoping that as they slept the spirits of Catherine and Arnaut would enter their bodies. Soon word of the miracle spread throughout the country. Visitors arrived by train from all over the continent. The existing hotels filled to capacity and new ones had to be built to accommodate the continuous stream of pilgrims. Additional priests were needed in Pau to meet the demand for marriages and the town swelled with intoxicated wedding guests reluctant to go home. Couples wishing to conceive a child started making love at night at the base of the statues. Soon couples, wishing to insure their union joined them. Strangers sought each other out during the day, waiting until nightfall to make love. Eventually the cultists grew too impatient to wait for nightfall and started making love during the day. In broad daylight, the square was strewn with naked bodies, orgies, and drunkenness. The fevered pitch grew, until one day, at the height of the frenzy, someone castrated the statue of Arnaut Vidal. The same person broke open the sarcophagus and made away with Arnaut's bones.

The mutilation had an immediately sobering effect. The magnetic aura surrounding the statues ceased and the naked revelers filed out of the square. It was only after the last of the pilgrims were gone and the square returned to quiet that one noticed the statue of Catherine de Monchensi. Gone was her smile. It had been replaced with a melancholic gaze. And the posture of her body, beneath the folds of drapery, suggested the languor of a convalescent.

from LOST CEILINGS
(1999)

*For a long time I saw no other sky than the ceiling
of this room where, from a chink of plaster, hung
the image of paradise….*

Philip Lamantia

WORLDS OF TIME

In the beginning she rose from the warm froth of the sea. The dust of stars settled in her girdle of Venus. A child's hand holding a shell holding the incorruptible music of eternity.

Warm and naked she rose. Draped in kelp and sailcloth. She alighted on the sands of time. A phantom horse in her belly.

Something new and unpredictable appeared every day. In pools of space she swam. A liquid shine in her eyes. An astronomer sighting new configurations among the already familiar.

One summer an immeasurable duration was born which the simple snapshots taken at the ocean failed to capture. On the dream plain she stood with her back to the light source. Facing the camera.

From a cavalcade of disembodied beings over her bed the writing came. From the forever. From an elegy in a country churchyard. The writing burst upon her. Awakening the melancholy that was her birthright.

In all that was struggling to attain form a migration of sparrows was sacrificed. As she made her way towards the spires of the magic city the tiny bones of a bird's wing were caught in her throat.

*

Now heaven draws farther and farther away. In Venus's looking glass the small approaches. The splintering of nerves occurs from morning to night and a knife falls in the path of whatever shines.

There is no time to sleep. In this frame she sits in bath water scented with semen and roses. Mad to know paradise between her legs. She opens the gate for the night gardener.

A fan unfurled. A fire stirred up with a poker. With one duty only and namely to make love. Through dark hours she is flushed with appetence.

Again and again. In a blue kimono echoing the sea she writes the same line. Over and over in the window the stars set to be the measure of time are invisible.

He is waiting. The phantom horse grazes in the corridors of time. Fueled with impatience she mounts him. To chase down the riverhead over the buildings.

*

Some day she will find something to rest on. The waves will bring an oracle. Walking into the surf in her Venusian skirts. A voice of wind and thunder will tell her where to go.

Winter will begin to show its influence. The hostile forces favored by the time will begin to advance. To perpetuate radiance she will retreat to a mountain fortress with four and twenty windows with a view of the magic city in every one.

That which is bright rises twice. In time the phantom horse may be reined with gold. The music transcribed from a spiral galaxy will no longer elude naming.

To breathe in time invigorated by grief. The imprint of a hand. The scribblings of the sky. It is written that the companion bird will once again sit on her shoulder.

The chanting of psalms at a steady rate fixes the hour. Before the film runs out her mind will be still for a while. In the Milky Way burning its inheritance she will chart the course of her ship.

Time buried. The pulverized relics of the past scattered like ashes. Through the portholes of the abyss she will look out at the imperishables. Forever.

MELANCHOLY LANGUAGE

Avalanche, entomb me in your fall!
Baudelaire

Wanting something. Nothing. Absence. Whiteness. Wanting a great annihilation of snows. Wanting something so beautiful as to close the office of the night. A dirge to play on the jukebox of the dispossessed.

*

At the end of the bar, snow is falling. In the windows on Spring Street, a black and white film of heavenly hosts is falling.   In slow motion, detached portions of the Milky Way have been falling for hours.

Here in limbo, a stone's throw from the river, a dull grief, a standstill that only the utmost whiteness will end.

A trip to the southern pole. Froth on the waves at sea. *Flying Cloud* rounding the horn in a print over the bar.   Her sails as white as the underside of an albatross, navigating archipelagos off Tierra del Fuego in her sleep.   The snowy cliffs of Isla Navarino filled with deep deposits of alluvial gold.

Old whaler's lore. Tales of old Manhattan sailors bottled in colored glass. My eyes in the mirror, contemplating their diminished fire

*

Absence. Whiteness. Wanting something so beautiful as to bury the city. Wanting to conceal the moon and stars behind a ceiling of alabaster. Absence.

*

Walking home. The white smoke drifting from the chimneys of the Federal houses. Wrought iron railings and sidewalks covered with snow. Flakes falling on a circus at the corner of Varick and Van Dam. Rare albino tigers and Himalayan elephants. Acrobats and trapeze artists leading a parade of children around a White parasol. A parade of children strewing petals around White Tara. Beckoning. Beckoning. Then dissolving.

*

Distances. Dispersing the clouds over my soul. Wanting something so beautiful as to take me out of this world. An avalanche to entomb me in its fall.

*

And still it comes down. The heavenly hosts fall in my window. At four A.M., paying homage to "The Prince of Poets," a candle burns beside a typewriter. Stilled by little deaths gnawing away. A photograph by Nadar. A trip book. A map of earth's last terrestrial frontier. The farthest, most desolate place. The continent of annihilating snows, avalanches, glaciers, and icebergs, drifting beneath a white sky.

*

Absence. Whiteness. Wanting something. Nothing. Wanting to fall into the consoling arms of sleep, and in falling, fall into a fleet of masts, pulling up anchor out of the harbor of losses. Wanting something so beautiful, as to sleep on the deck of *Flying Cloud*. Destined for Antarctic ice. Dreaming dancing lights of aura australis. Oblivious to the sound of the sea crashing against the bow. Oblivious to feet tapping to a concertina. Oblivious to my mantle of snow.

FROM SUITE OF DREAMS

Overture

With the first notes of the overture…wrapped in an old London Fog…high on the Palisades bare-ankle deep in the wet, summer grass…I lean on the hood of a car. Drowned at last… the voices of the day. At last…with sighs and yawns…the river flows into the night sea. Small craft and barges are buoyant candelabrum. An Italian ocean liner, like an anchored chandelier, beams its candles across black ripples.

But for the spirits inhabiting the ancient Weehawken cliffs, I stand alone, following the ladder of light…Up from the Hudson's surface…to the traffic on the West Side Highway… to the Empire State Building's white windows…to the movie screen high above everything….

THE SCHOLAR'S LIBRARY

A new bookstore has opened in one of the townhouses across the street from my building on Van Dam Street. Home from work, on a bright spring morning, I take the opportunity to visit the shop for the first time.

I climb the townhouse steps and peer into the front bay window. The books on display are scholarly, dealing with philosophy, history, geography and literary criticism.

I step inside. The shop is small. There are only a few bookcases and a counter, with an unattended cash register. There's an open door in the back of the shop. Through it, I see a library. Stacks and stacks of books climb from floor to ceiling, and large, mahogany desks extend to the far end of the room.

With some hesitation I enter. The library is crowded with greying scholars studying in hushed silence. Some look up and smile, as I walk between the desks. I sense that I'm enjoying a rare privilege.

Quite by accident, as I make my way to some particularly enticing-looking stacks, I step on an old gentleman's foot. He's not particularly alarmed. Rather than reprimand me, he questions me about the beat-up leather satchel I'm carrying. He wants to know if I know where it was made. He asks me, not so much out of curiosity, but to test my knowledge. "Seville," I say.

"Yes!" The old scholar is so delighted with my correct answer, he invites me to join him for lunch in the library dining room.

THE BLEECKER STREET CINEMA

Breathless and *The 400 Blows* are playing on a double bill at the Bleecker Street Cinema. I arrive early for the four o'clock showing of *Breathless*. I've made good time, walking in the bitter cold semi-darkness of the winter afternoon. I buy my ticket and climb upstairs to the lounge.

In front of one of the floor-to-ceiling windows, an attractive couple is already waiting. The young woman sits on a window seat, intermittently smoking a cigarette and looking at her fingernails. She is ultimately urban and cool. She's all in black — black leather jacket, mini skirt, black tights, black, stylish boots. She wears little makeup and is quite beautiful. Her pale features seem exotic — maybe Slavic. Her hair is light blonde, straight, shoulder length.

At her feet, her boyfriend is stretched out on the carpet, reading a magazine. He's boyishly handsome, with sandy blonde hair. He wears a black motorcycle jacket, Levi jeans and desert brown cowboy boots. He exudes the raw, masculine energy of the west. I have the impression that he just rode in from Montana.

I find it impossible to keep my eyes off the two. As I'm wishing I'd brought something along to read to otherwise absorb my attention, the doors for the four o'clock viewing open.

Inside, about thirty people — attendees of the two-fifteen showing of *The 400 Blows* — are seated. I take an aisle seat in the middle of the theatre. The attractive couple from the lounge sit down on the aisle to my left, three rows in front of me.

After a few minutes, the theatre darkens and *Breathless* begins. For a while I'm able to lose myself in the black and white Parisian streets, Jean Seberg's haircut and boatneck shirts and Belmondo's playful gangsterisms, but before long, the totally cool couple, who've been all over each other, making out since *Breathless* started, have my full attention.

Towards the end of the film, just as the Paris police are about to arrest Belmondo, the couple remove what little clothes they're still wearing. They lay down in the aisle and start to make love.

Their spontaneity is greeted with enthusiasm by everyone in the movie house. The French film aficionados gather around the lovers and cheer them on. They throw dollar bills at their naked bodies and release silver, helium-filled pillows into the air.

I become so aroused, I have to leave the Bleecker Street Cinema and forgo *The 400 Blows*.

THE CHESTNUT MARE

At the tail end of a procession on Carmine Street, beside a flower-draped float bearing a life-size likeness of the Virgin, I ride side-saddle in an honor guard. Since the start of the procession, the August sky has been overcast and threatening. Now as the statue of the Virgin is about to be carried into Our Lady of Pompeii Church, thunder begins to roar in the distance.

I dismount from my Chestnut mare and tie her reins to an iron post. The ceremony installing the Virgin beside the altar takes longer than expected. When I'm finally back out on the street, my mare is agitated from the combination of heat and thunder. I try to calm her with soothing words and strokes. I remount her and lead her south on Carmine, lightening cracking the sky.

We're turning onto Sixth Avenue from Bedford, when the storms hits full force. We're caught in a torrential downpour and hurricane winds. I sense how frightened my mare is. She rears up on her hind legs and shakes her head, wildly. To gain control, I throw my left leg over her back and assume a full-saddle position. When I do this, it makes her more excited and sets her off at break-neck speed. I'm convinced she's going to throw me. It takes every bit of horsemanship I have, to slow her to a gallop.

Once things have stabilized, we're able to halt. I dismount and cover her with a yellow rain parka. Then slowly, very slowly, I walk her to her stable on North Moore.

THE GREEN NOTEBOOK

It's a warm, Sunday afternoon in July. The Catholic Archdiocese is throwing a party in honor of Pope John Paul II's visit to the city. Fifth Avenue, from 46th to 59th Streets is one giant street fair. Thousands of people inch their way past stalls selling gyros, religious articles, stationery supplies, T shirts, sunglasses, guitars, radios, beer, zeppole and cannoli.

The pope, all in white, stands in front of St. Patrick's Cathedral, waving to the crowd. Joining him on the steps are city and church officials, a high school band, and a prize-winning chorus from all five boroughs singing Polish folk songs.

Twirlers hurl chromium batons into the air. Little children bring the pope trophies from the street fair on silk pillows. One by one, to the sound of thunderous applause, the pope bends down to receive each gift and kiss each child.

I wander through the festival hoping to find a new notebook at one of the stalls selling stationery supplies. At 56th Street, I spot a beautiful specimen. It's bound in knobby, dark green leather. I pick it up to examine it more closely and smell the leather. It's a nice size, about four by six inches. When I open it to see if the paper is lined or unlined, I read "from The Path of Perfection, translated from the Pali by Juan Mascaro."

Instead of a notebook I've found a beautiful, leather-bound, pocket edition of *The Dhammapada*.

from NOCTURNES

To soothe him in his longing,
And inspire him there's the Night.

Novalis

1

It's eleven o'clock. A bare wolf's tooth bites into the darkness, emptying the streets of all but the most devout. From the tallest spires of glass, aluminum and steel, the last prayers of the day sound. *Bind my hands.* *Sanctify my heart.* A formal pause extends its wings in the icy silence, followed by prayers from the smaller towers. Across the blue, jewel-encrusted masts of the city, voices echo voices with the same assaulting plea. *Take me.* *Guide me.* *Illuminate me.* Holy night. *Take me as I am.*

2

Falling, falling, falling, from such great distance. Shrouded in a layer of dense white cloud. From some sidereal desert falling. Falling in folded wings of snow, the night plants a moistened kiss on the window, awakening toxic fragrances of hot house blooms. Along the inner sill, bright, conspicuously displayed reproductive organs of jasmine and gardenia are the sweetest offerings. To hunger after forgetfulness. In the deep, dark center lies the succulent fruit.

In the deep, dark center, what bed of litanies unfolds before the night? The hands of what Perseus remove the chains, opening penetrations into a landscape of supplicating flesh? What prayer, whispered to invoke oblivion, rises like a bird from the heart?

5

Grotto of night. Now the door to seclusion opens. Arched recess lit by the silver egg of the moon. To enter the threatening darkness. Desire. To see the marvels lying within. The frozen stalactites on the ceiling. The boat of Morpheus, ready to go.

See the animal land. Permanent rose horses. Feathered green anacondas. The doe-skinned female lion leading her suspended white mate on a leash. Her marcasite eyes are the authors of Chaos, its portal defended with inflexible rigor.

See the flora in the narrow strip of fields between the walls of the cave and the banks of the underground stream. The flowering tops of pistillate hemp plants. The red, bell-shaped petals and black, shiny berries of deadly night shade. Oozing capsules of opium poppy, filling and emptying the mind of pleasure, sadness and disgust.

Should we go? Or stay in the land of Pan? Its luminous rocks and thrones on the sand, draped with pastel scarves. A land of muscular flutists and warm, creamy emissions on the beds. A land without enemies, ruled by the enormous appetite of dreams. A land without time to define the parameters of anything

6

Waiting in a flowing, flower print dress. Through the open summer window, the strong hands of the night reach in, and slowly, one-by-one, unfasten the buttons down to the waist. After a thunderstorm, the metallic perfume of rain predominates and the soft hiss of cars coursing over wet pavement.

How welcome the calm. The respite from the dance. Day's chorus line of skeletons. Just for the moment, benevolent gargoyles guard the city from perches high atop a deco skyscraper. Wise and heavy with patience. Their hearts are fortified by hope.

Stirring in a glass of dry white wine, a cool fingertip. An old album by Orpheus on the record player. Music for lyre placed among the stars. Music for waiting to be filled with light.

7

There at their beginning. At the end of Leroy Street, a boy in a blue shirt gathered from the distances between the stars, lends his shoulder to a girl on fire. In an aureole of lamplight. Grace. Beauty of form.

With every wave from a passing craft, an anchored sailboat buoys up and down, entering them with wind chimes and Japanese lanterns. Lifting, raising their eyes, they can almost see themselves in the sky over the river.

The easy entry of the foreordained. Lovers climbing a ladder of white silk cord, from the dock, to the other side of the night.

Time slakes its thirst on Labor Day. In the hot, humid air, breezes weave between them. Entwined spasms of body and soul. In a transport.

10

Hunted all day by the wings of an enormous bird of prey, the old heart of the world stumbles towards the cover of sleep. The long battle of hours ends in blood in the warehouse windows facing west. The sun's happy departure sets off rows of fire.

For the elect now a shower of arrows over the empty streets signal the beginning. A white transparent dress embroidered with moonstones comes out of the closet, replacing a suit of camouflage. Out of the deep vault of the city, six white horses rise to the new land of tireless worship. The least resistance is obscured by the sound of the soul's inner and outer strings tuned to perfection. As Night, the Prince of Light, unlocks the double gates in his ceiling, an invigorating aquatic melody covers asphalt and cobblestones.

LOST CEILINGS

Mirror, mirror on the floor. How the sharp, silver slivers reflect the truest likeness of the soul. Splintered, insignificant pieces, on the edge of this world, a little haunted tonight

The four white walls of the hermitage surround.   A polar diorama.   A landscape   of ice, interrupted by a pocket of desk lamplight

In the hand of an anchorite, a lantern.   Fra Angelico's *Annunciation*.   The Horse Nebula, composed of gas and dust. The Pyramids of Giza. Picture postcards, circumscribed by amber glow. Picture postcards, left behind at the entrance to an uncharted network of inland seas

Soaring wings over choppy waters. Away from this world, the genie of the alphabet rises out of the typewriter with a rosary of fire. Twenty-six beads of blood for twenty-six letters. To fly in the face of finitude

Half obscured, the telephone receiver lies on its side, under a Mexican shawl, muffling its sound. Such solitude as afflicts the room, tilted on an angle. Unassailed on the cusp of darkness

The bookcase, in the cold thin clouds, is a heavenly trove of torches. Burning pages. Paths and spirals. Labyrinths. Lighting the way to a desert birthplace. Far, far away from this world

In the midst of an ocean of sand. The genie of the alphabet rises out of the typewriter with his horn of plenty. Serenading the lost ceiling of stars with high notes

WHITE EVENING

Now exquisite quiet lulls the buildings in the weight of snow   falling in front of windows on the avenue   a tender desolation kindles my eyes   the frozen correspondence of the stars

Above the snow   and the snow below   bowing to kiss the city's hardened breast. Her lurid flesh as white as a supplicating Magdalene's beneath the streetlamps

Nothing.   The season.   The evening.   And the drifts   effacing time   spent with my monotonous soliloquy

Going home   to wine's internal summer   burning in the absence of prayerful rites like a candle in the cavity of an ice sculpture

A MAP OF THE HEAVENS

Compiled and drawn in the Cartographic Division of the National Geographic Society, my umbilical to the sky rolls back from the wall. So many holes and tears made in its corners over the years, it can hardly hold a thumbtack or a nail. But still, on the faded indigo field are all the brightest stars. Sirius, Vega, and Betelgeuse. Alpha and Beta Crucis. White souls whose magnitudes have dimmed with age.

Below me, the Lords of Night take pains to lay out objects in a hexagonal pattern, on my bed. Through a parting in the canopy, I can see multi-colored scarves, a crystal skull, obsidian bowls and knives, a ruby-glass carafe, a kif pipe in a pouch made of leather and ocelot fur, with dangling silver charms. Will the Lords succeed in instigating chaos tonight? Will they distract me? Entice me? Subdue me? Ensnare me? Will they, with offerings in hand, climb all the steps of my pyramid? All the way to the temple at top, where I sit at my desk, with the desk lamp on, gazing at a window on the universe.

A trail of smoke that is the Milky Way. The desert wastes of Mars. Seas and mountains of the Moon. The whirling storms of Jupiter. Saturn coated with ice. Serpens. Draco. Pegasus. The Lady Chained. Orion the Magnificent. Eighty-eight constellations, with thin red lines connecting the principal stars of each. Forming skeletons of the signs of the zodiac. Luminous nebulae. The Northern Sky. The Southern Sky. The entire celestial globe mapped in two hemispheres, with 1,971 stars shown as they would be seen by naked eyes from the poles.

Pushing upward through the jungle. The sound of machetes hacking entangled vines. At first a violet velvet turban appears through the tops of the trees. Then a shoulder caped in black satin. Slowly and determinedly, my would-be suitors, my initiators of the fall of light, climb the steps of my pyramid. Sixty-seven. Sixty-eight. Sixty-nine. Will they succeed tonight in filling me with too much of myself? Will they? Before the tide rises, can I swim away through my conduit to heaven?

LA BELLE INDIFFÉRENCE

The night despairs. I'm alone beneath
the random arrangement of constellations and I don't care

The present's here taking me by the throat. How well the emptiness becomes me, as the great ship departs full-blown through a lid in my skull. A rusted mariner's compass. In the basin of my fountain dead leaves lie under a layer of autumn frost. Listless and numb. I bare the marks of this raw and drifting continent

The night despairs of looking at itself. In the mirror I see the red eyes of my demon behind me and I don't care

I come and go down here in the stupefying barrens of creation where a brutal hand has tossed the stars. A severed statue wing on a path leveled by fire. I stand still. Undisturbed by the blades wedged in my back. A frozen moon ghost broken by exhaustion. I'm exiled from the city of marvels

The night despairs. Lame like a lion with glass in its paw. I'm turned to stone and I don't care

Angel haunted music plays. Far from here the absolute pitch of the pure and tempered scale hovers over cliffs over the river. Every second my heart used to beat, waiting for an aria to take me to a flower bed circled with candlelight. Now I'm deaf to the voices mounting. Under my ceiling a pendulum swings

The night despairs of the hours to come. I take my wounded light to sleep and I don't care

RAIN

for Trid

A cold Tuesday morning in February. In my dream, Cinemabilia — the film book and memorabilia shop — is located on a narrow street in the Marrakesh souk. Ernest, the owner — looking every bit like Sidney Greenstreet in *Casablanca*, wearing a fez and a white linen suit — is sitting with his young Arab assistant in the entranceway. The shop is small, sparsely filled.

I'm on my way to the food quarter to buy bread and goat cheese for lunch. I wave to Ernest as I pass the shop. He invites me in. There's only one movie poster on the walls, one bin of black and white stills, one case holding a few books and items of memorabilia.

We chat idly about current films and the superior quality of their predecessors. At the end of the conversation, He tells me about a Moroccan radio station.

> *Rain, rain, rain, _____*
> *I don't mind.*
> *Shine, shine, shine, _____*
> *The weather's fine.*
>
> *I can show you that when it starts*
> *   to rain,*
> *ev-'ry thing's the same.*
> *I can show you, _____*
> *I can show you.*

The song on the radio plays in a jukebox, worlds away in a coffee shop. Of all that's gone, I keep the cold winter rain against the windows, an anthology of French Symbolist poetry, a corduroy jacket, the proper positioning of the wrist while holding a cigarette and laughter, always laughter.

Barely does the morning light filter through the bamboo slats of my shade. The steam heat bangs and hisses in the radiator. The news comes on, and the Map of the Heavens rolls back from the wall.

I get dressed, have a cup of coffee and a cigarette. I throw on a trench coat, grab an umbrella and step outside to navigate my way around the trucks on Van Dam Street. At the corner, I hail a cab. Slowly, through the traffic, it makes its way up Sixth Avenue to 13th Street.

"Silents, please!" reads the greeting over Cinemabilia's entrance. Gloria Swanson, Harold Lloyd, Lon Chaney, Louise Brooks — their blown-up faces look down from the posters on the wall behind the raised platform where the owner's desk is located. I'm expecting to see Ernest wearing a fez and a white suit this morning, and when I hear that he won't be coming in because he's caught the flu, I'm disappointed. He's left word that I'm to continue writing and typing capsule book descriptions for our forthcoming catalog, *Men and Women Behind the Camera*.

The suspension of disbelief. Edison's kinetoscope. The magic lantern. Muybridge. Méliès. Anita Loos. DeMille. Dorothy Arzner. Griffith. Buster Keaton. Hitchcock. Truffaut.

All day the rain comes down. The radio plays classical music on WQXR. Terry talks rock n'roll business on the phone. Ann catches up on the bills. Ira and David sort through stills. I write and type, and from time to time, I look up at the poster across the room from where I'm sitting. I look up from my little desk on the platform. I look up from the books and electric typewriter into Monica Vitti's blank, existential stare. I look up and wonder why Antonioni called his film *The Red Desert*.

Was Antonioni referring to the emotional effect of color in the film? Did he wish to create an association with passion and blood? Was desert meant to refer to a landscape, i.e. the industrial landscape of northern Italy, or was it a state of mind? In San Francisco, the film played at a time when Antonioni momentarily rivaled Fellini as my favorite filmmaker. The theatre was a beautifully maintained Art Deco shrine. Monica Vitti had red hair and wore simple black heels and a grey overcoat.

Simple black heels. A railroad yard. Crossing the tracks to rendezvous with her lover.

Marlene Dietrich taking off her heels to follow Gary Cooper into the desert.

The walls and the surrounding desert are rust red in Marrakesh. The French girls there have red henna highlights in their hair. We arrived at sunset in a horse-drawn carriage and went immediately to the *Djemma el Fna* — the centuries-old square in the medina, teeming in the ochre glow with food stalls, acrobats, water-sellers, bird acts, snake charmers, scribes and musicians. We bought packets of kif and watched the sun set in red, from the roof of the hotel.

If the rain comes,
they run and hide their heads,
they might as well be dead;
If the rain comes,
if the rain comes _____

At seven o'clock we close the shop. I walk down lower Fifth Avenue in the rain. The wet rustle of leaves forms a protective ceiling overhead. Few people are willing to brave the weather. On Washington Square North, I see Olivia de Havilland, running down the stairs of *The Heiress*'s townhouse to a waiting carriage and Montgomery Clift.

Turning south on MacDougal, I pick up falafel at Mamoun's and hurry home — into a pair of black, silk pajama pants and a striped sailor shirt, to sail away on the surface of the immense accumulation of rain. So much rain, lower Manhattan has become a small city of canals, and my apartment is a houseboat anchored in an isolated lagoon.

After dinner I call my little sister.

"I had a dream that Mommy and I were shopping in the souk in Marrakesh. We walked into a movie theatre. You were there, behind the candy counter, selling beautiful striped sailor shirts for a dollar each. I bought two. A white one with red stripes and a red one with white stripes. You were also selling mohair sweaters. Powder blue. Lavender. And mint green. The kind Mommy liked to wear in the winter.

We were hungry, so I left you and Mommy in the movie theatre and went back onto the street to buy goat cheese and bread for lunch. I saw Ernest sitting in a little shop. It was the new Marrakesh branch of Cinemabilia. Then the radio woke me, playing 'Rain.' Trid, what album is 'Rain' on?"

"It's not on an album."

"Are you sure? Not eve an English album? I thought it was on the English *Revolver*. The one with John, Paul, George and Ringo on the cover in white doctor's coats, holding decapitated baby dolls."

"That was the American *Yesterday and Today*. It was only in the stores for a day before it was recalled. Then it was reissued with a new cover with the boys wearing beige suits and turtlenecks."

"So 'Rain' isn't on any album?"

"No, it's on a forty-five. It's the flip side of 'Paperback Writer.'"

THE SLEEPWALKER'S ETERNITY

In abundance of yellow light she moves, accompanied by an angel with rainbow wings. She moves without the old fears of self-immolation. Forever shaded, her eyes guard against intrusions.

In her city, the doors fly open. The windows fly open. Endangered birds build nests at the top of the skyscrapers. The future emerges from secret refuges on every corner. Gypsies read cards foretelling days of exalted, trance-inducing music played for friends who are always near.

And only someone bearing fruit. Someone born to complete her. A burning object to whom she might cling. Lies on the bed in her red room.

FROM *BODY OF WATER* (2008)

Let night come on bells end the day
The days go by me still I stay....
Apollinaire

BODY OF WATER

Standing by a body of water. Moving or standing still.
In the dark green depths my soul finds its own level

Lost in a mirror of infinite margins. Ever
sounding. On and on. Perpetual arms pull me
under light's silver sheets. Tossed with wind
and waves.   Where a coiled muscle gives up
a perfect word. I come with only a fever to offer
far from the dried carnations in summer's throat
and certain birds that pierce the air with an agonizing
cry. I come to wash and be clean. To drown in my immensity

Baptized by a spray of distant sky. In sympathetic
response. The surface repeats the hypnotic patterns
of my longing. Again and again. Swimming out
to the breaking pages before me. With only
a parched fountain to offer. Far from the sun's
entrenched lullaby of insect music and the worried
sleep that parts with a film of sweat and dust
I come to be carried away through the charitable
doors that open on the shore

Standing by a body of water. Moving or standing still.
In the dark green depths my soul finds its own level

NINE CARD SPREAD

There's a deck of cards face down on the table

Will the night's apocalyptic starfish still swim in the stream
            circling the lady's waist?
Will her garden always yield pearls of jellied moon
            ripped from the side of florescent sharks?
Will her walls anchored in the sea floor uphold trellises
            laced with continuous light?

There's a deck of cards face down on the table

Will the lady find herself hanging upside down in a window
            on the other side of the sun?
Will the fool in her fall on the swords protruding
            from the drapes of the covetous city's drawing room?
Will the pride of lions in her shoulders bear the weight
            of her own dark angel wounded in the rain?

It's in the cards. It's not in the cards
the heart of a mandolin hums in the hand
the jacks are holding oracle bones
in the pockets of their suits. It's in the cards
it's not in the cards. Past and sudden
revelations bring the house tumbling down
around the Queen of Clubs so pressed for time
It's in the cards. It's not in the cards
the present portends stasis and flush sails
picking up wind in the eyes of diamonds
looking out on the joker's wild eternity

There's a deck of cards face down on the table

Will the bridge spanning the abyss be there going and coming
        from the lady's armchair to the rim of the crowd?
Will she divine a way with more than string or ribbon
        to harness the dragon appearing in her field?
Will she learn to dance with her head brushing the clouds
        and her feet patterning figure eights in clover?

There's a deck of cards face down on the table

THE GREEN HARMONICA

The mouth begins a movement
along the orbits of celestial bodies
along the roof of the house of angels
along the line of least resistance
notes correspond with the heart's sudden ocean
conquering the walls
the breath inhales
a chord of joy and relief
unlocks the lid of longing
along the length of the green harmonica
green channels of distance flooded

The mouth begins a movement
a moment of hesitation
takes off with the speed of transient stars
and souls pursue their instinctive sail of the universe
green glasses shatter. green bar lights make the mirrors shine
green of the concrete floor. the breath exhales
trailed by a string of the brightest lanterns
breath that reaches the darkest corners of the room
breaks in the hollows between the reeds

Green wings beating against the ceiling
along the boulevards of the Milky Way
along the length of the green harmonica

OUT OF THE BLUE

The horses that carry me   have brought me
this far   as I reach for the sun   a skywriting plane
comes flying   out of the blue   a script of cloud
a wisp of hand   holding an old card of fortune
through a rip in the roof of the tent   oracles come flying

For my horses   flutes and drums have always
urged them over wastelands   they've carried my luggage
this far   full of prayer beads and photographs
they've carried me to all that's yet to be   bowed heads
in a circle of sawdust   heavy with blankets of roses
as I reach for the sun   their hearts are open   but
their yellow wings are slack with age   any moment
ancestral music   will call them away

As I watch them leave the spotlight   a fresh mount
is needed to lift me   above the circus   above
the tiers of clowns   the sermons of fire and gnashing teeth
the dust blown in the eyes of angels   on the midway
a million tours of blind alleys   the bells that ring three times a day
reminding me to atone   above the safety nets and fleeing distractions
up to all that's yet to be

As I watch my horses leave the spotlight
a white steed comes   flying in the tail winds
of the skywriting plane   flying with the grace
and muscle of Al Borak   Black Beauty   Pegasus
Marengo   Rosinante   Trigger   Traveller
Silver   Native Dancer   Sea Biscuit   and Secretariat
a new horse comes   out of the blue   to lift me

up to the message in the clouds —

Though escape by land and sea is blocked
still there's a way through the sky

up to the old card of fortune —

Mount spirit wander at your ease

as I reach for the sun
through a rip in the roof of the tent
up to all that's yet to be

FLYING NOWHERE

Head winds and rain
from New York to Shannon
but we're flying. Nowhere
don't bother packing
you won't need a toothbrush
we're flying. *Par Avion*

Watch the wide rover's wings
during takeoff
you don't have to fasten your seatbelt
if you're stuck on the aisle
and can't see the city
the dazzling lights
of Rockaway Boulevard
will always be there

We're flying. Nowhere

Over the ocean
lines from Yeats and O'Casey
are scrawled on the backs of the seats
even in Economy
the Chieftains are inside the headphones
and Van Morrison's latest CD
if you didn't bring valium
you're not going to need it

We're flying. Nowhere

Aer Lingus has duty-free shopping, in flight
Waterford crystal and Chanel No. 5
if you don't care for Jameson's

you can ask for a Guinness
if you don't like lasagna
there's chicken pot pie
if you don't like the movie
you don't have to watch it

We're flying. Nowhere
Nowhere. Nowhere
flying nowhere
nowhere. Nowhere. *Par Avion*

Pockets of turbulence may occur
the nose may take a dive
 clouds may darken the pilot's vision
and throw the plane off course
if you don't have a rosary
you can count on your fingers
if your life jacket's missing
you've still got a prayer

We're flying. Nowhere

Coming in for the landing
the plane glides like a sleigh
on a snow surface of clouds
to the right catch a glimpse
of the green coast of Ireland
keep calm and grip the arm rests
when the wheels hit the runway
and you'll be fine

We're flying. Nowhere

Going through customs
officials at Shannon
will want to see your passport
if the old one's expired
and you forgot to get a new one
or you left it behind in the kitchen
with the camera and the Baedeker's
don't worry

We're flying. Nowhere
Nowhere. Nowhere
flying nowhere
nowhere. Nowhere. *Par Avion*

Notebooks on the high street in Skibbereen
a sweater to bring home for Joe
the view of the stars from the crater
at Liss Ard
on your very last day
sitting sadly by the sea in Castletownshend
if you don't want to say goodbye
you won't have to

We're flying. Nowhere

Head winds and rain
from New York to Shannon
but we're flying. Nowhere
don't bother packing
you won't need a toothbrush
we're flying. *Par Avion*

Nowhere. Nowhere
flying nowhere
nowhere. Nowhere. *Par Avion*

SLEEPING GYPSY

The tongue is unsatisfied   firebird sweets
a morsel   a taste of carrion   sleep
desire will have its form
and beasts go forth   as in a dream
your belly warm as birth
the newborn skulls of coyotes ripping through
like egg teeth in a dance of bones
of spinning light
the frantic tongue
insatiable

Sleeping gypsy scatter your horns
the animal parts
the dangling limbs of tapestries
prey of the huntsman   St. Julian
his relentless bow and divinity for madness
his angel ecstasy for animals
blood pudding   firebird sweets

Sleeping gypsy
it's not the time for siestas of lions
desire will be your beast
and its jaws roll around a moan
of ageless stone
primeval prankster
fork your tongue
like a dragon
spit

STAR PARTY

Following the curve of the Dipper's handle
warm summer torsos are high overhead
in the azure fields phantom fingers
pluck the strings of a harp
how can you keep your feet on the ground
with the Scorpion's heart the rival of Mars
it's a perfect night for a party

Moonless and clear the Milky Way
rises as smoke from a million candles
the head of Our Lady of Labyrinths
crowned with a wreath of asters
how can you shield your eyes from the mirror
with the Arrow striking a golden apple
it's a perfect night for a party

Get out your star maps and binoculars
we're going to stay out all night long
on the rooftops in Central Park
what good is heaven for
if you don't look at the sky

Thirty thousand light years from here
the history of an ancient race is written
on the dome of the Great Blue Mosque
a hero lies upside down in a burning shirt
how can you sleep through the overture of the universe
with crystal birds pursuing the Lion
it's a perfect night for a party

Get out your telescopes and naked eyes
we're going to stay out all night long
in the backyards in the campgrounds
what good is heaven for
what good is heaven for
what good is heaven for
if you don't look at the sky
look at the sky
look at the sky
look at the sky

BLUE GIRL

Weary of waiting, blue girl. Following the map
of a vanished sea. Blue lights in the harbor
blue sails carry you through twilights
obscuring your lodestar with dusk. Dark-adapted eyes
in the period of blindness, between the gods departed
and the gods yet to come, all that is rare and excellent
furnish your happy isle's watchtower of white
all that you seek. All the soul's companions
the music of grazing horses plays on the shore

Shaped by the charity of the firmament, blue girl
gold scales begin to rise. Over the water, at the edge
of the dream line, prevailing winds favor a crossing
go on ahead. The deepest chamber of the night
will restore your exhausted wings. Go on ahead
there, there is pleasing variety in the moon and stars
awaiting your imprint. The shimmer of leaves
breathes a song without words
and corals lie lost from the track of the world

ARIA

With bewitching sweetness
the deep song of sleep
takes you under
her Spanish shawl

I'm left with your soul's breath
the smell of sex
and the meteorites at the window
casting a shower of diamonds
over our skin

Unconquerable isometric crystals
older than the earth's mantle
older than the moon's crust
dispersing prismatic colors
forged in the fires of the first casting mold

Victorious dark-eyed sleep
embraces you with embroidered flowers
and the deep song
of subterranean waterfalls

I run my hand across your chest
It comes away with diamond dust
destined to be scattered
wide among the stars when we die
returning to our source in the sky

SEVEN VEILS

Rain, rain sweeps through the streets
as they grow dim
the face of the moon is lost in the clouds
under the veil

A castle keep
the thousand tears of the forest
the window of an exiled queen
dark as the sun sunk under the earth
with her heart pierced through
she paces back and forth
breathing a thin air of hope

Rain, rain shrouds the buildings
in ghostly mist
ankle wings speed me along
under the veil

A horde of sparrows
the high green hedge of a garden
mazes of passages making it hard
for the songs to find their way
to the entrance from the center
music rises like a golden flood
over centuries of night

Rain, rain makes the heavens clear
relieving the sobs of broken angels
from a high perch the eyes take measure
under the veil

A viper in hiding
bound with ropes and cords
desire's delirious spring
is locked within
longing to make it to the far world
beyond the aloofness of memory
molting in the frame of an antique mirror

Rain, rain the wind is strong
the branches bend low to their limit
light pours out of a buttonhole
under the veil

The blazing sails of a ship
the seaworthy masts of a caravel
heading out of the harbor
with an unfamiliar sextant
without a guide to the chaos of the sky
without a mission or goods to transport
sailing without reason to sail

Rain, rain heavier now
running in sheets off the rooftops
life's secret soul wells up
under the veil

The steadfast light of a hermit's lamp
fueling the emptiness
with impatient brightness
in the desert desolate and lonely
a flame held close to the chest
a season of victories waiting
in the shadow of hostile cliffs

Rain, rain here to stay
filling the holes from here to the river
a silent corridor lined with lions
under the veil

The evening dancer
emerging from a vermilion tent
with slippers of gold and a ruby choker
at the invitation of the infinite she dances
for him only will the wild dogs stay away
beyond the campsite in the pitch blackness
with the perils of cold sleep

Rain, rain makes a soft asylum
shielding me from a tireless hunter
nothing touches the nerve ends of the universe
under the veil

A map of the night in autumn
a jaded Pegasus in holding
marked by an absence of magnitude
still with one blow of his hoof
fountains spring forth
stable doors come down
and flight through a field of Arabian stars begins

OPEN WINDOW

The air is cool. Coming
with the tourmaline sea
into my symphonic interior
caresses. Both yours
and the breeze's lingering
longer days of dazzling
light flood the room
above the Avenue of Palms

A bed with the imprint
of your body on it. Sugar almonds
on a silver tray. Posing as if for a painting
before a Moorish screen. Four goldfish swim
in a bowl on fire. My skin is blushing
pink like a battle of roses

After a bath. The charged
idleness accompanying
your absence wraps around me
in the silk of a white kimono
in the frame of the open
window. I can see my buoyant
heart. Sailing the Mediterranean
with a wind caught
under its wings

MY MACUMBA

A bird crashed out of the sky. his spirit lodged in my throat
I could feel it choking me. and I couldn't breathe

Macumbeira spread out her shells on the table

"My daughter," she told me
"The hand of your Mother, Iemanja, will hold you
The Queen of the sea is your saint
You'll fall down. But when the spirit leaves you
it will be as though he never existed
Go and bathe in the essence
of white medicinal roses
then make your appeal to the saint."

Waves broke into stallions. mottled grey in the night
I lit a candle and walked to the edge of the ocean
pouring wine for the goddess

A bird cried out in my throat to be free

I fell down. and when his spirit left me
My innocence. my self-confidence returned

SPELLBOUND

Spellbound. Words escape me. Going out
as if a flame. Extinguished. My capacity
to want anything

In this transport the temperature is dropping
on the top floor of the walk up. The mane
of a nameless horse. Tossed back
among the waves in your eyes. The blue heaven
and the open sea bringing the sundered night
to an end. In the web of separate things
the flight of the night's lost bird is ending
on the most remote corner of the world
an explosion in me. Lying in the ashes
of a dress. My ember wings make a last fluttering gasp
knowing they've seen enough. Downstairs
the linoleum is covered with bleeding prayer rugs
and the walls and ceilings take on a crimson glow
No other hand but yours reaches out of the sky-drifts
to check the fire. No other hand

Spellbound. Words escape me. Going out
as if a flame. Extinguished. My capacity
to want anything

In this transport the temperature is dropping
in a cold ray of moonlight
on your bed
I pass away
annihilated
from head to foot
in the fortress
of your aloneness

114

THE MAN WITH THE SCARLET KNEE BANDS

Heart be still
be quiet

Though impressions
burn in you
like fires
out of control

Be still
be quiet

Throw buckets of ice
on the hot stones
you set out so feverishly
to walk upon

Be calm
be confident in your goal

The man with the scarlet knee bands will come

The man will come
to kiss your hands
and bathe your feet
with water
from an invisible world

Be still

Be full of hope
and expectations
and mindful
of the mystery of things

For he will come
down a long, long stairwell of approach

He will come
the man with the scarlet knee bands will come

To join you
and caress you
with a yellow light
that fills your holes

THE SOVEREIGNTY OF THE CLOUDS

Up from idle gazing. A gliding hawk leads me
towards the sky's consensual arms. Floating
in a supine meadow. a red tail. Lifts me up
to summer's cumulus reign of horses
levitating on a blue canvas. Bending their long white necks
beneath coronets of green and purple grapes
baby's breath and Queen Anne's lace

O seasonal arousal of cirrus galleons. Sails of silk
blooms of foxglove. Phlox. *Lunaria annua.* Dahlias
doves. Snowdrops. Owls. Polar bears. Peacocks. Monkeys
yarrow. Carnations. Buildings. Bunnies. Japanese white spirea
sports cars. Eyebright. Cockatoos. Tigers. Tents
continents. Elephants. Castles and canyons
dispensing an elixir of time extracted

A THOUSAND YEARS

How goes the night?
how goes the watch
as midnight approaches?
in the storm waves of
 the sky
the moon beats a gnarled fist
on her old yellow drum
a thousand years
have passed away
a thousand years
are yet to come

How goes the night?
how goes the watch?
a lone sailboat makes its way
through tolling towers
sounded by the motion of the sea
a thousand years
fill the hold with dust and desire
a thousand years
of wasted wings to set free

Fragile the wilderness
the skeleton bells ring
for eternal return
another March breeze
blowing across the planet
another life with new idols
and the same concerns

How goes the night?
how goes the watch?
flood waters swallow enfeebled horses
fallen from the cracks in the dome
a thousand years of races
in the funeral beds
a thousand years of fits and starts
before we're home

How goes the night?
how goes the watch?
in the end there's a full single sail
propelled by its own will
a thousand years
bring a pale beacon
with the coming dawn
a thousand years
of moving forward and standing still

Fragile the wilderness
the skeleton bells ring
for eternal return
another March breeze
blowing across the planet
another life with new idols
and the same concerns

SEA FEVER

Under the bridge the water is full of ships
if it could quake my heart would wrest away
from its guards and assume a throne
as tall as a topmast moving out to sea. Beneath
a crown of stars hymnal sails in the ascendant
night's moist consummate air carrying me
to a wilderness beach where the rest of me waits
beside your side

A tide of horses swims through the swollen
black lanes to the moon. A weight of wanting
roped to their backs

At a dead gallop. The waves would break me
if I could open in your wide white arms
a prodigal mermaid with eyes on fire. Buoyed
by love's wild wings. Eastward leaning
in the phosphorous sky where the ocean gathers high
towards heaven. My summer skin
of silk and mother-of-pearl drinks
in the still asylum of a blue sound

DARK SKIES

How far they are from paradise. In the grass
at the end of the parking lot. A handful of magi
rowing a barque through a neglected passage
of longitude. Dressed like mendicants. Fallen
from an elevated oasis. Without turbans of gold
or embroidered coats. Only faded linen
replicas of leopard skins

Behind them the eastern night. The guard dogs
at the burial grounds barking into the empty tombs
where the stars of summer were interred. In rows
of glass coffins. Stars from the pale blue wings
of a swan. Stars to move the rocks and trees
with songs. The dolphin's stars

Now missing from the fresco over the city
the lion's silver goblet overturned. Where last
the supper sat. A crystal cob-webbed chandelier
hangs in an infirmary of pigments. No wind
no current stirs the still life. Just bowls of dust
flooded with light and scraps uneaten

The spots of a thousand eyes
dropping like flies
dropping like flies

MOVING STAR

Lightning striking   fluorescent serpents
This wave of hot breath over my spine

Let's have another drink

while the hailstones and demon rain
bounce off the corrugated roadhouse roof

Let's swallow our spirits
and obliterate the night

*

> *Moving star*
> *bird of fire*
> *open your wings across the sky*

A white hot poker
this fervent tongue
is burning a hole in my spine

> *O ceaseless opal phoenix, sing!*

Let's have another drink

while the thunder roars
and spreads its dread
a hundred miles around

Let's put another quarter in the jukebox

*

Moving star
bird of fire
your light is a voice

Oblivion

your light is a song

utter oblivion

blowing the veils
away from my eyes

obliterated in a long black tunnel of clouds
we drove the car   weird insect harmonies
currents of air   violent, vertical movements
of heat escaping the ground surface
the shock to the eyes   bloody green toads
and dismembered lizards falling out of the sky
an army of locusts alighting on the windshield
we drove the car on   into the dark Dakota night
longing   longing for unnamable things

*

Lightning striking   fluorescent serpents

These sudden waves of hot breath over the spine

Let's have another drink

while the thunder roars

Let's have another drink

full of smoke   noise   and confusion

TOMB FOR OPHELIA

Gently, lifeless. After his play. Her toy in blood
no longer harms the river nesting in orisons
Though day it is. The wild white roses of her face
and palms collect the bright stagnation of anointed moons
more tears in floods. More sighing and lamenting
did she see his antic disposition. Did her heart
beat down between her legs. Did he lie there

Gently, lifeless. The pendant boughs of willow
couldn't bear the weight of her. Holding columbines
and cornflowers. Rosemary and rue.   Grieving
without judgment. Divided from herself.   The greying
grace of her gown buoying a sacrificial bride
the black clouds of his mourning suit in the center
of her eyes. Fixed on a heaven too high to climb

DOOR TO DOOR

Now I lay me down   weary of reading
indecipherable maps   relieved of the weight of amulets
and timepieces   I lay me down   on cool white sheets
on a pillow with a key of gold   I lay me down to open
the doors where all that is stalled lifts off in dreams

A door opens on Lorca   standing with his back
to the camera in a courtyard in Spain   wings protruding
from the shoulders of his white linen suit   on the front lawn
of my childhood home a door opens on maple trees
filled with light   I sing to them and angels appear
in the upper branches   in the deserts of Venus
a door opens on a pale horse turning pink in the rosy glow
of the setting sun   all that is stalled lifts off in dreams
birds of ruby glass alight on the pilings of a pier
over the Hudson   a door opens on the palms
of my hands scarred with hearts and wands   crosses
glyphs and planets   assuring my good fortune
to get lost in a movie palace   circling a sarcophagus
filled with sand from the Valley of the Kings
deep in outer space   a door opens on Neil Young
the sky pilot flying from point to point to fire the stars
with a gas torch igniter   and all that is stalled
lifts off in dreams

On a bed rimmed with flowers and the yellow pollen
that glistens on my skin in the dark   I lay me down
on cool white sheets   on a pillow with a key of gold
I lay me down to open the doors where all that is stalled
lifts off in dreams

A door opens on a courtyard   deep in outer space
in the palms of my hands   the night opens at last

THE ENIGMA OF BUSTER KEATON

1.

I looked out the window of the train into the pink-golden sands
of the desert. Into the blank incandescent infinity
looking at a sunset on Venus. The book on my lap
was open to The Enigma of Buster Keaton —
the small white Egyptian in a linen suit. Walking
through the snow with a straw boater and cane

Palm trees. Swimming pools. The back lots of the studios
the endless possibilities of silence

I looked out the window
into the eyes of the mystery
on a platform
outside the high Spanish ceilings
of Union Station

2.

A crowd of photographers and reporters surrounded him
in his snow shoes. A school of parasites on the gills
of an angel fish. Light bulbs flashed. The exposure
caused discomfort. He was moving fast. But
not fast enough to elude them

"Excuse me, sir, but can you explain
your divine comic invention
improvisation

and spontaneity?"

"Why don't you use a script?"

"How do you come up with all the gadgets?"

"Can you explain your lucidity?"

He turned with his usual grace. It was vaguely
reminiscent. He tried to place his feet on the ground
the gravity wasn't there

"Excuse me, sirs. I beg you to leave me alone
I've awoken from sleep into a nightmare
too vast and unimaginative. Please, my eyes
are painful. The high Spanish ceilings are calm
but I can't see the cherubs gathering about the rafters
I'm suspended in vertigo. My car is waiting
please, I can't keep it waiting

To answer your questions before I go

I use the silence precisely
naturally and intuitively."

3.

I took a cab to the tall iron gates and proceeded
up the driveway leading to the villa. Weeds
were trimmed between the stones under my feet
and ivy grew over the toy house for the children
in the moonlight the vegetation was lush and alive
invigorated by a Santa Ana wind

I knocked on the door. It opened on a young blond
about to run her silver fox into the manicured night

"He's waiting for you in his bedroom," she said
then ran across the lawn

Potted palms. Persian rugs. The endless procession
of extras dancing to a jazz band

4.

A maid took my wrap. I was directed to a table
with champagne and hors d'ouevres.   It was hard to guess
the number of people under the chandeliers
the ballroom was filled to capacity

I sipped my drink and observed the sparks going off
before me. Floor-length gowns sequined with rubies
and diamonds. Falling into tuxedoed arms of perfumed volcanoes

The bandleader called for an intermission

I made my way up the wide congested stairwell

There were rooms leading off the landing like voyages
in one men played pool
in another women talked of jewels and fame

5.

A stream of candlelight swam out from a crack beneath the door
at the end of the hallway. I walked over and knocked
it opened slightly. Inside I could see The Enigma
of Buster Keaton in a linen suit playing with a set
of trains on the floor. The snow fell all around. A thin
layer settled on the tops of the furniture

I stood there wondering about his ability to travel
he sensed my presence behind him and turned around
sending a sliver of dry ice into my bloodstream
with his wide pharaonic gaze

The train set was located in the middle of the room
they were band new. French passenger trains
driving through snow storms in the Alps
with a strong light on the silver engine to guide the way
beside a royal blue butterfly umbrella lying on the floor

He picked it up and walked towards the open windows
a wind caught under the flaps of his pockets
and lifted him off the floor into a series of somersaults

"Where do you go when you're not dreaming?
when you're not in love
when the oppressive contagion of reality engulfs you?"

He took my hand and led me through the movements

I, FELLINI

8½
in the sky
over the scaffolding
for the space ship launch

My happiness
is this bullhorn
and straw fedora
in the blistering sun
of Cinecitta

On the birthday
of Studio 5's youngest grip
my friends
you've toasted me
and my new film
with spumante in paper cups
and in return
I'd like to say

Grazie amici!

I, Fellini
in my forty-third year
of beautiful confusion
have been hired
to shoot a masterpiece
and I will
riddle the Sistine ceiling
with buckshot

Kidding, only kidding

I, Fellini
will shoot Mastroianni
in a perfectly cut Milanese suit

Mastroianni
with greying hair
and sad dark circles
under his eyes -
the Adonis of despair -
I will shoot Mastroianni
in such a light
women the world over
will want him
in their Roman beds
Chinese beds
beds in the U.S.A.
even outer space

I, Fellini
who am nothing
without my crew
the actors and actresses
all the extras
the extravagant
black and white palette
of Gherardi
di Venanzo's magic lens
and primo maestro
Nino Rota's score -
to let you know
the circus
of the spheres

I, Fellini
who am nothing
if not my own creation
will shoot Mastroianni
into the stratosphere
in film number eight
and a half

Si, otto e mezzo

Primo, The White Sheik
then *I, Vitelloni*
La Strada
Il Bidone
Le notti di Cabiria
La Dolce Vita
and *The Temptations of Dr. Antonio* -
as you know
a complete film
within *Boccaccio '70*
Variety Lights I don't count
I shared the director's credit
with Lattuada

Le mezzo?

Agenzia matrimoniale
from *Amore in Citta*, 1953
only thirty-two minutes

I, Fellini
who am nothing
without you

have been hired
to shoot a masterpiece
and I will
lift it off the storyboards
from the comic strip
in my mind -
Mandrake
and Mastroianni
up into the stratosphere

Soon, today, now

We can start whenever you like
just say the magic words -
asa nisi masa -
and we'll all be rich
to each and every one
an Alfa Romeo
four cases of spumante
and an apartment
on the Via Veneto

Your part, Marcello?
you ask about your part

I see you like me
in a state of beautiful confusion
following a nuclear disaster
a director, terrified
of making his next film
boarding a spaceship -
the new Noah's ark -
with friends and associates
you'll fly to Mars

and marry a nice Martian girl -
una bella ragazza
with fishy scales
and a single eye in her forehead
Well, maybe not
maybe three eyes
in her forehead
who knows?
I'm still working
on the concept

I see you making love
to your Martian bride
but it won't be enough
it's never enough
we always want more
don't we *amico*?

You'll have a harem
of exotic space girls -
Anouk, Sandra,
my lovely Saraghina -
on Christmas Eve
in the Martian snow
you'll walk through the door
with presents under your arms
for all of them
they'll bathe you
and caress you
but it won't be enough
it's never enough

You'll sit by a fountain
listening to your inner voice

just like me
you'll hear nothing
niente, niente, niente

I've said enough
let's begin
before we destroy
this film
with talk

At the end, we'll begin at the end

Maurice, my ringleader
have you got your top hat?

Eccellente!

Now hoist me up on the dolly
let's have the clowns
with their instruments -
tuba, clarinet, French horn -
and the little boy
with his flute
in his white cape and cap

I want them in the middle
All the actors and actresses
all in white
position yourselves
along the rim of the circus ring
everyone hold hands
and spread out together

Maurice, when I give you the sign
you're to look
straight into the camera
and say -
"Life is a great white movie screen
Let's step into it together!"

Marcello, when you hear
those words
you'll step up on the rim
and join the parade

Are we ready?

Asa nisi masa

All quiet on the set

Azione!

RED HILLS AND SKY

In the sky I am walking
a black bird
flying over Ghost Ranch
loud and raw
under my feet
the red hills still
touch my heart
as they never touched
anyone else's

I saw something
I wanted to say

In the miles
and miles
of badlands
all the earth colors
of the painter's palette
were out there –
the light Naples' yellow
to the ochres
orange, red
and purple earth –
even the soft
earth green

I saw something
I wanted to say

Driving past
on a trip

to the Navajo country
clean white bones
and bare red hills
rolled away
beyond the windows
of the Model A Ford –
the easiest car
I ever had
to work in –
in the lonely
feeling place
called Ghost Ranch

I saw something
I wanted to say

I unbolted
the driver's seat
turned it around
and painted
with a 30 x 40 canvas
on the back seats
until four
in the afternoon
when the bees
were going home

I painted
a black bird
flying between the arms
of two red hills
reaching out
to the brilliant sky
and holding it

BYRON'S TIME SHEET

Good Lord! Byron's set sail. Never to return
one lame foot planted firmly on the deck
never to return. A dismal shroud
draped on Dover's cliffs. Dalliance with him
is involuntary sport.   But he doesn't get paid
for loving his sister, the likeness of himself
not with fame springing overnight and Caroline Lamb's
scene at Lady Heathcote's ball. He doesn't get paid
for that.   Not with Dr. Polidori and a staff
of retainers fleeing the snub of Mayfair's beau monde
He doesn't get paid for that. No.

*He gets paid for clerking in a bookstore. That's
what he gets paid for.   At twenty-eight he's going grey
but he doesn't get paid for that. He's clocked
fourteen hours on his time sheet for one entire year!
But he'll never get paid for it. No. He'll never get paid!*

Good Lord! Byron's thrown himself on a chambermaid
in Brussels.   But he doesn't get paid for that
what he earned from *Childe Harold*, Cantos I & II,
was spent in a fortnight. Never to return
friendships with him are always passions
but he doesn't get paid for sharing a boat
with Percy Bysshe in the turbulent waves
on Lake Geneva. No. He doesn't get paid
for being fortified with brandy and laudanum
and stepping into the dungeon at the Castle of Chillon
No. He doesn't get paid for that.

Good Lord! Byron's appetites have pursued him
over the Alps.   Never to return. His travelling coach
is equipped with a wash tub.   But he doesn't get paid
for that. Not with Burke's sublime in the sheer drop
before him and avalanches every five minutes
he doesn't get paid for that.   He doesn't get paid
for two years in Venice in the Palazzo Moncenigo
on the Grand Canal. No.   Not when he's standing
on the Bridge of Sighs with the Occident in one hand
and a turban in the other. He doesn't get paid for that.

He gets paid for clerking in a bookstore. That's
what he gets paid for.   At thirty-two he's going grey
but he doesn't get paid for that.   He's clocked
fourteen hours on his time sheet for one entire year!
But he'll never get paid for it. No. He'll never get paid!

Good Lord! Byron's set to work on *Don Juan,*
"a little finely facetious upon everything." But
he won't get paid for it. Not if he's taken as his mistress
the wife of an Italian count. No. Not if he's storing guns
for the Carbonari. He doesn't get paid for that
He doesn't get paid for yachting with the English colony
at Pisa or witnessing the burning of Shelley's body
on the beach. No.   He doesn't get paid for swimming
out to his schooner, the *Bolivar,* to exorcise
his violent remorse. No. He doesn't get paid for that.

Good Lord! Byron's landed in Missolonghi. Never to return.
One lame foot planted firmly on the ground. Never to return.
He's been named by unanimous vote
to the Greek Committee.   But he doesn't get paid
for that. He doesn't get paid for advancing loans
to the patriots and parading in native dress. No

He doesn't get paid for riding out in the rain
and returning drenched in an open boat. He doesn't
get paid for throwing himself at destiny and leaving
his heart behind. No. He doesn't get paid for that.

He gets paid for clerking in a bookstore. That's
what he gets paid for.   At thirty-six he's going grey
but he doesn't get paid for that.   He's clocked
fourteen hours on his time sheet for one entire year!
but he'll never get paid for it. No. He'll never get paid!

K E R O U A C

I had nothing   but I had a grey tee shirt
and I ironed on black velvet letters

K   E   R   O   U   A   C

I had nothing   I had four walls on St. Marks Place
a bottle of Calvados   and the silence of the universe
I had nothing   but I had you

From sea to shining sea   east to west   north to south
Atlantic   Pacific   Arctic   Antarctic   the Indian Ocean
and the eighth mar incognito   over   under   inside
and out   beyond everything   I had you   I had words
lines   and paragraphs rushing down mountainsides
high above the timber line   from Desolation Peak
to 242 choruses of blues for the Buddha and fellaheen
of Mexico City and every other place   I had your
footprints on the beach in Tangiers   your palm print
on the wheel of impermanence   your dreams of long
childhood walks under the old trees of New England
your athlete's body   your flannel shirts
your handsome face on a fire escape on E. 7th Street
just before the invocation of Duluoz   inhaling
one last Lucky Strike for the pent-up   aching
restless road   farewell subterraneans and water towers
of Manhattan   it was time for all that coming back
to America   the Lincoln Tunnel   oil tanks
and anemic skies in New Jersey   Route 80
over the Delaware   the road unraveling   the road
sufficient unto itself   a twentieth century
pilgrim's way   a home for the tathagata passing

through the railroad earth   the gas station night
the bebop radio wail of Charlie Parker's saxophone
clear across Kansas   to San Francisco   the little alley
off Market Street   Tokay in a paper bag
at the mouth of Bixby Canyon   Big Sur's ocean roar
of vowel sounds   from the far side of eternity
the waves laying better than a thousand transcendental
diamonds of compassion at your feet   even to the end
I had you   to the maenads of fame   tearing
you to pieces   in the glow of the television set
in Florida   to what's buried in Lowell's Edson Cemetery
Ti Jean   nothing's buried there   the dust
of your sacred bleeding catholic heart   with that
of the holy ghost   and certain mad and driven
saints   has been placed among the stars

I had nothing   but I had a grey tee shirt   and I ironed
on black velvet letters

K   E   R   O   U   A   C

BLUE TANGO SHOES

From New York to London and back again
the courses of our cryptic mythologies
soar in midflight   converge   and go their separate ways
in a bookstore window in Buenos Aires
you saw sparkling blue tango shoes
and thought of the mariner offshore in the distance
adrift from the gold and silver canvas of your world
that fits so perfectly - a shirt of star field cloth

Always there's a porcelain angel   in the pitch and roll of my study
the blue tango shoes take their place
among the saints and rosaries
brought back from your Pythagorean travels
notebooks like this new one from the Argentine
a box of twenty-five eggs of semi-precious stone
and the last armless soldier from a box of one hundred
we bought on Second Avenue

Miniature blue tango shoes   blue roses and feathers on the toes
blue ankle straps   from Borges' city
where you prowled the streets   looking for treasures to stock the hold
of my heart   and in return this poem —
a vial of pale green seawater
to wear around your neck

FROM MOON MUSIC

1

In a courtyard on the moon
the dust blows
over the bottom of the sea
to silence her broken cords
the dust blows

At the bottom of the sea
the milky neck and torso
of a lost guitar
over the frets and hollow
the dust blows.

Luna maria, luna maria
luna maria, luna maria

In a courtyard on the moon
waiting for the one
to hold her
the guitar cries
from the bottom of the sea

The guitar cries for fingers
long and tapering,
to make her music
in a courtyard on the moon
the guitar cries

Luna maria, luna maria
luna maria, luna maria

2

Draped in the sonata
of summer's end
the full emptiness of the moon
spills out of a grand piano
diagrammed over the water

A wave as warm
as the sex of the moon
carries her through channels
of sea hands
assaulting her negligee's
light-blossoming florescence
dying away

In the spent bleaching
of teeth, foam, seaweed tresses
and ivory nakedness
the moon looks up
at what fashioned her at first –
an extended movement
of tonic and dominant keys

3

I've come out early tonight
leaning over my balcony
lowering myself over the railing
to hear your music
fill the tide pools

I've come out early
in a pale blue gown
wearing the silver and feldspar
you gave me
and the earrings of white coral

Like my path now
on your surface
I tossed and turned all day
in my bedroom

"You'll feel rain again,"
my seahorse said. "You'll see.
The ocean will wet
your thighs with his waves."

I've come out early tonight
with pearls in my hair
searching the beaches,
extending a moon bow
showing my ring finger
free of my promise to Mars

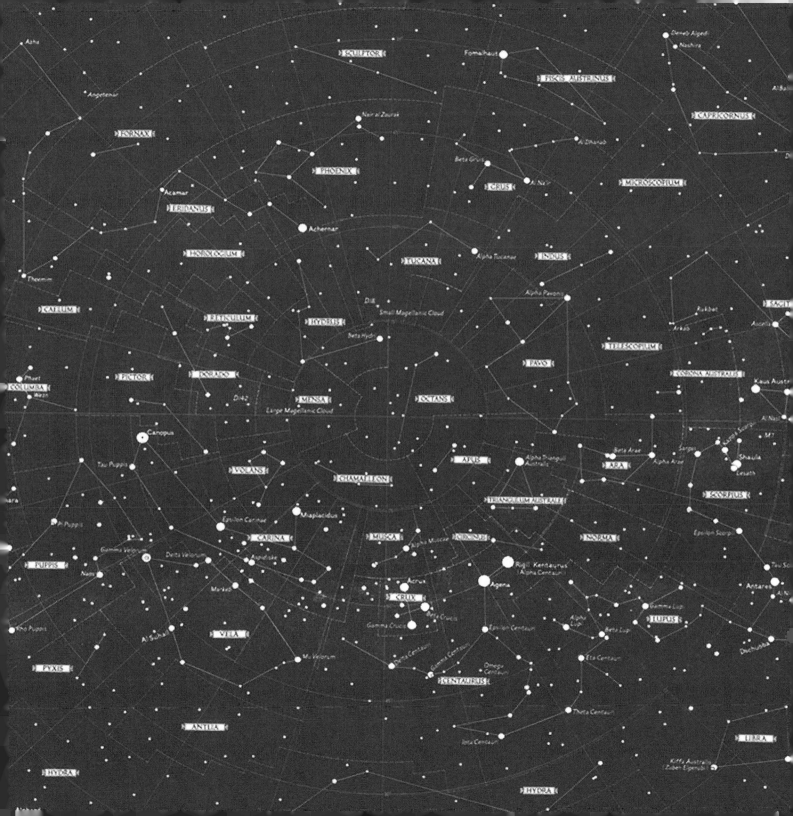

from *KNOCK*
(2016)

Travel makes one modest. You see what a tiny place you occupy in the world.

Gustave Flaubert

FROM KNOCK OF HOLLYWOOD

In old Victorians   syringes clogged the drains of claw-footed bathtubs
along the Panhandle   amber petals bloomed in the Tiffany lamps
their trunks & branches carved of bronze   to replicate knots of redwood
uprooted   to fringed   art nouveau parlors   sprouting peacock feathers

Along the Panhandle   amber petals bloomed in the Tiffany lamps
liquidating Hollywood shoulder pads   thrift stores made everyone a star
uprooted   to fringed   art nouveau parlors   sprouting peacock feathers
for glamour shots   sequined slippers & deco greyhounds vogued in windows

Liquidating Hollywood shoulder pads   thrift stores made everyone a star
from the Presidio   & Alcatraz   back lit by views of the Golden Gate
for glamour shots   sequined slippers & deco greyhounds vogued in windows
we got stoned   & hitched to Mt. Tamalpais   the eucalyptus you know

From the Presidio   & Alcatraz   back lit by views of the Golden Gate
the Grateful Dead & Hot Tuna played Winterland   New Year's Eve 1970
we got stoned   & hitched to Mt. Tamalpais   the eucalyptus you know
in old Victorians   syringes clogged the drains of claw-footed bathtubs

Home to the Chumash & Tonga   Los Angeles was claimed for Spain in 1542
Juan Rodriguez Cabrillo planted the flag   in the middle of a religious trance
a vision of the HOLYWOOD sign appeared   in a Moroccan-bound journal
sent to the king   via two-masted caravel   with flasks of Santa Ana wind

Juan Rodriguez Cabrillo planted the flag   in the middle of a religious trance
a substitute for the Virgin was Queen of Angels   on Paramount's back lots
sent to the king   via two-masted caravel   with flasks of Santa Ana wind
rich   from growing roses & oranges   raising cattle   & avoiding poison oak

A substitute for the Virgin was Queen of Angels   on Paramount's back lots
the trail led by bus or hearse   to the site where the Black Dahlia was found
rich   from growing roses & oranges   raising cattle   & avoiding poison oak
someone killed her   cut her torso in half   & gave her a smile from ear to ear

The trail led by bus or hearse   to the site where the Black Dahlia was found
there the Tonga took a last stand   drawing the mark of Zorro in sand
someone killed her   cut her torso in half   & gave her a smile from ear to ear
home to the Chumash & Tonga   Los Angeles was claimed for Spain in 1542

Nebraska at night   tracking Pawnee footprints   & escaped Spanish horses
along the braided river   stars thrived in satellite clusters   Ogallala   Sutherland
the rush of waters from Wyoming & Colorado   to caress in North Platte
Ground Control to Major Tom   Commencing countdown   engines on (five   four   three)*

Along the braided river   stars thrived in satellite clusters   Ogallala   Sutherland
space on earth   sweet darkness   from the passenger seat of the panel truck
Ground Control to Major Tom   Commencing countdown   engines on (five   four   three)
in the headlights on Route 80   oncoming miles left behind   in cowboy land

Space on earth   sweet darkness   from the passenger seat of the panel truck
Led Zeppelin's "Stairway to Heaven"   beamed down   on silos of soy & grain
in the headlights on Route 80   oncoming miles left behind   in cowboy land
the deaths of Hendrix & Joplin   when love's blossom opened in slow motion

Led Zeppelin's "Stairway to Heaven"   beamed down   on silos of soy & grain
between here & there   angels sat at the controls   how else to explain the radio
the deaths of Hendrix & Joplin   when love's blossom opened in slow motion
Nebraska at night   tracking Pawnee footprints   & escaped Spanish horses

*David Bowie

155

In 1832   Sauk & Fox made their first land concessions   west of the Mississippi
for forty barrels of salt   forty barrels of tobacco   & blacksmithing services
vivid hallucinations resulted   from the ingestion of belladonna   by bikers
parked by a fountain   in the evening light of a fertile valley town in eastern Iowa

For forty barrels of salt   forty barrels of tobacco   & blacksmithing services
someone's old lady told me he saw a woman in front of a dressing mirror   in a slip
parked by a fountain   in the evening light of a fertile valley town in eastern Iowa
they put us up   gave us weed   & fixed the panel truck's gear box   for nothing

Someone's old lady told me he saw a woman in front of a dressing mirror   in a slip
she worked for a chiropractor   & was studying to be one   when he touched her
they put us up   gave us weed   & fixed the panel truck's gear box   for nothing
137 years after the Black Hawk War   he felt empty space between her shoulders

She worked for a chiropractor   & was studying to be one   when he touched her
rubbing ointment into a disc in her backbone   she flew to a gathering of witches
137 years after the Black Hawk War   he felt empty space between her shoulders
in 1832   Sauk & Fox made their first land concessions   west of the Mississippi

FROM KNOCK OF TIJUANA

Ay! Ay! Ay! Ay! Ay! Ay! Ay! Ay! South of the border down Mexico way...*
Orson Welles looked like hell in *Touch of Evil* planting evidence as always
Dietrich told him to lay off the hooch & candy bars wearing chandelier earrings
in the single camera three-minute opening sequence film noir swan-songed

Orson Welles looked like hell in *Touch of Evil* planting evidence as always
the American bride of a Mexican narcotics enforcer was raped in a Texas motel
in the single camera three-minute opening sequence film noir swan-songed
then she whispered mañana & drew beaded curtains & the stars came out to play

The American bride of a Mexican narcotics enforcer was raped in a Texas motel
they held her down & put a needle in her arm as the radio drowned the menace
then she whispered mañana & drew beaded curtains & the stars came out to play
for it was fiesta the gun had been stolen in Quinlan's soiled topcoat & fedora

They held her down & put a needle in her arm as the radio drowned the menace
later the Captain's cane was found near an oil field he died in a wastewater pool
for it was fiesta the gun had been stolen in Quinlan's soiled topcoat & fedora
Ay! Ay! Ay! Ay! Ay! Ay! Ay! Ay! South of the border down Mexico way....

*Gene Autry

Time   time   time   time   the burden of it   marking of the passage of it
at interval ends   stelae were erected & inscribed   with the age of the moon
at Chichén Itzá   serpents slithered up the steps of the pyramid   to lick the sun
giving life to time   until the next equinox   & Quetzalcoatl's green descending

At interval ends   stelae were erected & inscribed   with the age of the moon
presiding over period endings   the gods set down their heavy   sandbags of time
giving life to time   until the next equinox   & Quetzalcoatl's green descending
years of bad crops & wars were seen   in the windows of the Venus Observatory

Presiding over period endings   the gods set down their heavy   sandbags of time
each day was divine   a divine pair of gods   in the Mayan highlands of Yucatan
years of bad crops & wars were seen   in the windows of the Venus Observatory
the red orb was a star   a planet   a jaguar's eye   a stone sphere on the ball courts

Each day was divine   a divine pair of gods   in the Mayan highlands of Yucatan
through eternity   by relays of bearers carried   with straps across their foreheads
the red orb was a star   a planet   a jaguar's eye   a stone sphere on the ball courts
time   time   time   time   the burden of it   marking of the passage of it

A poet of statues & nocturnes   Villaurrutia spoke of his studio to Octavio Paz
"I have to construct this artificial refuge for myself   in order to endure Mexico"*
a set from one of Cocteau's films   *Blood of the Poet* or *The Testament of Orpheus*
kept him company   with black drapes   & the bleeding eyes of a sculpted head

"I have to construct this artificial refuge for myself   in order to endure Mexico"
oblivion's oblivion   sleep walking   both asleep and awake   I silently cross the sunken city
kept him company   with black drapes   & the bleeding eyes of a sculpted head
the others   the men & women he passed on the street   didn't appear in his work

Oblivion's oblivion   sleep walking   both asleep and awake   I silently cross the sunken city
ignoring newsstands   buses   barbershops   & the excavation of ancient ruins
the others   the men & women he passed on the street   didn't appear in his work
touching in darkness   the immaterial rose   the rose of rosy fingernails clawing the surface

Ignoring newsstands   buses   barbershops   & the excavation of ancient ruins
he was born to be a savage aesthete   not eating cheap   authentic   street food
touching in darkness   the immaterial rose   the rose of rosy fingernails clawing the surface
a poet of statues & nocturnes   Villaurrutia spoke of his studio to Octavio Paz

*Xavier Villaurrutia

Just like the earth   the night was a jaguar   chipping away at paint
Rahon's *Crystals in Space* canvased the walls of a cave   as black as black
the jungles south of Mexico City   flowered & swelled   between her legs
a cobalt blue song for a friend   conceived in the San Ángel neighborhood

Rahon's *Crystals in Space* canvased the walls of a cave   as black as black
one of Kahlo's eyebrows was monkey hair   the other borrowed from a cat
a cobalt blue song for a friend   conceived in the San Ángel neighborhood
at the top of a Ferris wheel   lights came on when their corsets were exchanged

One of Kahlo's eyebrows was monkey hair   the other borrowed from a cat
wrapped in a harlequin's blanket   Varo searched for amulets on the sidewalk
at the top of a Ferris wheel   lights came on when their corsets were exchanged
for every woman with the head of an owl   she sketched dragonflies in charcoal

Wrapped in a harlequin's blanket   Varo searched for amulets on the sidewalk
alchemical glyphs marked the door   Carrington's easily identified dawn inn
for every woman with the head of an owl   she sketched dragonflies in charcoal
just like the earth   the night was a jaguar   chipping away at paint

FROM KNOCK OF THE ATLANTIC

From Jacksonville   at 30° latitude   we began the crossing to Casablanca
the Jugolinija's Zvir embraced the high seas   above the Puerto Rican trench
seagulls hovered for miles   waiting for scraps of salami   & crusts of bread
starboard   port & bow   dolphins jumped in the air   playing high speed

The Jugolinija's Zvir embraced the high seas   above the Puerto Rican trench
I could feel the upwelling & sinking down   away from the land-locked world
starboard   port & bow   dolphins jumped in the air   playing high speed
for a short time we had land signals   & Brando didn't show for his Oscar

I could feel the upwelling & sinking down   away from the land-locked world
The Godfather was a master class   but he didn't give a damn about a gold icon
for a short time we had land signals   & Brando didn't show for his Oscar
most of our time was spent reading & smoking on deck   a pull for suicides

The Godfather was a master class   but he didn't give a damn about a gold icon
we made friends with Carlton   a Connecticut Indian   traveling   in the bar
most of our time was spent reading & smoking on deck   a pull for suicides
from Jacksonville   at 30° latitude   we began the crossing to Casablanca

At any given longitude   moonrise or moonset   Beethoven's *Ode to Joy* unfurled
in mid ocean   stars etched sails on my breast plate   gazing north in late winter
I mounted Taurus   & held the faceted crystal fingers   of the Gemini twins
without distinction between cloud or crest   the railing braced me   holding on

In mid ocean   stars etched sails on my breast plate   gazing north in late winter
I never escaped the sound of the waves   more than a cradlesong to the inner ear
without distinction between cloud or crest   the railing braced me   holding on
to steer the big wheel   after dinner the Captain invited us to the observation deck

I never escaped the sound of the waves   more than a cradlesong to the inner ear
the Zvir was equipped for electronic navigation   but celestial guidance was fixed
to steer the big wheel   after dinner the Captain invited us to the observation deck
very old school   as every seaman worth his weight   is in love   with Polaris

The Zvir was equipped for electronic navigation   but celestial guidance was fixed
compass   quadrant & sextant   he kept the tools of his student days   at hand
very old school   as every seaman worth his weight   is in love   with Polaris
at any given longitude   moonrise or moonset   Beethoven's *Ode to Joy* unfurled

The entire time   you rose and fell behind my eyes   when sighting whitecaps
few & far between   the sting of tears   when I came   wrapped in a wave
such were the correspondences between us & an ocean   of perfumed mackerel
after lunch   your semen was sea foam   slipping between my legs in the cabin

Few & far between   the sting of tears   when I came   wrapped in a wave
my safari pants from Modell's Sporting Goods   way downtown   on the floor
after lunch   your semen was sea foam   slipping between my legs in the cabin
sailors spun myths from chaos on leave   from smoky dens   I longed to enter

My safari pants from Modell's Sporting Goods   way downtown   on the floor
between the sheets   we simulated the foreplay of Coney Island's beluga whales
sailors spun myths from chaos on leave   from smoky dens   I longed to enter
every port of you   was a port in the world   laid out for horizontal exploration

Between the sheets   we simulated the foreplay of Coney Island's beluga whales
sating the veins of Argonauts   sea currents mapped the route to the holy grail
every port of you   was a port in the world   laid out for horizontal exploration
the entire time   you rose and fell behind my eyes   when sighting whitecaps

Only once did we pass another ship   another freighter from Rijeka   perhaps
it was exciting   but when it disappeared   we had the Atlantic to ourselves   again
I read *Nicholas and Alexandra*   in a volume of condensed novels   in the bar
at 32° longitude   Tsarevich Alexei suffered from hemophilia & Lenin plotted

It was exciting   but when it disappeared   we had the Atlantic to ourselves   again
on a bright morning   the calm surface was a pearl image of my soul   wandering
at 32° longitude   Tsarevich Alexei suffered from hemophilia & Lenin plotted
Nicholas insisted on autocracy   Alexandra turned to Rasputin to heal her boy

On a bright morning   the calm surface was a pearl image of my soul   wandering
Alexei sported sailor suits   in official photos   his sisters wore white lace dresses
Nicholas insisted on autocracy   Alexandra turned to Rasputin to heal her boy
a droplet in the storm of revolution   historic writings etched on Neva ice

Alexei sported sailor suits   in official photos   his sisters wore white lace dresses
they gathered diamonds & sewed them into their pockets   never suspecting the end
a droplet in the storm of revolution   historic writings etched on Neva ice
only once did we pass another ship   another freighter from Rijeka   perhaps

FROM KNOCK OF GIZA

We spent hours in the *Djemaa el Fna*   searching for Valentino's silent sheik
Marrakesh nights   shrilled to a blue cacophony   tattooed with henna stars
hands of musicians   water sellers & story tellers   were equally constellated
in back allies of the Medina   we bought sebsis & wax paper packets of kif

Marrakesh nights   shrilled to a blue cacophony   tattooed with henna stars
haggling over bridal jewelry   rugs   & djellabas   my passport was stolen
in back allies of the Medina   we bought sebsis & wax paper packets of kif
with my silver-studded   leather satchel   in the interconnecting passageways

Haggling over bridal jewelry   rugs   & djellabas   my passport was stolen
for a temporary replacement   the police told me to go to the office in Rabat
with my silver-studded   leather satchel   in the interconnecting passageways
the spectacle was viewed   from the open-air café   on the bus station's roof

For a temporary replacement   the police told me to go to the office in Rabat
until I could get there   they signed & stamped a paper   ensuring easy travel
the spectacle was viewed   from the open-air café   on the bus station's roof
we spent hours in the Djemaa El Fna   searching for Valentino's silent sheik

The Great Pyramids were accessible   by taxi   from the window grill
our hotel looked down on sandbags   barricading government offices
after the Yom Kippur War   Egyptian agents were solicitous   in the cafés
we didn't give a religion   on visa forms   or in conversations with the natives

Our hotel looked down on sandbags   barricading government offices
I should have avoided the breakfast tea   for a Pepsi   at the Cairo Hilton
we didn't give a religion   on visa forms   or in conversations with the natives
at the base of Khufu's pyramid   I became separated from the others

I should have avoided the breakfast tea   for a Pepsi   at the Cairo Hilton
with a hand to my forehead   I laid in my djellaba   weak from diarrhea
at the base of Khufu's pyramid   I became separated from the others
a strong force was present   Osiris beaming me up to his night boat

With a hand to my forehead   I laid in my djellaba   weak from diarrhea
on the modern road   businessmen liked night clubs   lit with neon pasties
a strong force was present   Osiris beaming me up to his night boat
the Great Pyramids were accessible   by taxi   from the window grill

Rimbaud or the madness of dogs   I remember the beads were cobalt blue
the nights of his violent worries   & the azure splinters in his eyes   alleys
of a weight good in the hand   the fortune he never amassed from guns
as brave as falcons   on the old wall surrounding the city   four in a row

The nights of his violent worries   & the azure splinters in his eyes   alleys
I searched for him in the Motown   the Coca Cola Cafe   built in Egyptian style
as brave as falcons   on the old wall surrounding the city   four in a row
guarding the five gates of Harar   the five gates of Islam   still closed at night

I searched for him in the Motown   the Coca Cola Cafe   built in Egyptian style
he wore a white skull cap   on the porch with his servant   & sacks of coffee
guarding the five gates of Harar   the five gates of Islam   still closed at night
to keep packs of hyenas at bay   a man fed them strips of meat on sticks

He wore a white skull cap   on the porch with his servant   & sacks of coffee
there were one hundred camels in the square   emaciated from desert famine
to keep packs of hyenas at bay   a man fed them strips of meat on sticks
Rimbaud or the madness of dogs   I remember the beads were cobalt blue

We rented a car from the King of Nairobi & drove south   through the Rift Valley
Zebras & impalas grazed on grass   as old as three million years of shifting plates
in Olduvai Gorge   the Leakey's excavated bones of the earliest human species
overseeing our entrance to the Serengeti plains   a maned lion with a wounded paw

Zebra & impalas grazed on grass   as old as three million yeas of shifting plates
at sunset   towering heads of giraffes   bent over acacia trees   for dinner
overseeing our entrance to the Serengeti plains   a maned lion with a wounded paw
limping into the future   with its wildlife threatened   by poaching & sport

At sunset   towering heads of giraffes   bent over acacia trees   for dinner
we pitched our tent & built a fire   under the first sighting of the Southern Cross
limping into the future   with its wildlife threatened   by poaching & sport
the howls of the big cats & their prey   instrumented a nightly orchestra of fear

We pitched our tent & built a fire   under the first sighting of the Southern Cross
elephants moved into camp   almost trampling us to death   with the fauna
the howls of the big cats & their prey   instrumented a nightly orchestra of fear
we rented a car from the King of Nairobi & drove south   through the Rift Valley

FROM KNOCK OF SAN TROPEZ

At bus stops from Seville to Cordoba   espadrilles displaced hard-packed sand
grit ground its way into hair & teeth   in the provincial capital of Al-Andalus
under the caliphate of Al-Hakam II   a *saeta* arrow pierced Manolete's suit of lights
blood red where his groin had been pink & gold   gorged by Idleroz's filed horns

Grit ground its way into hair & teeth   in the provincial capital of Al-Andalus
mannequins of boys & girls in First Communion dress   lined avenues of windows
blood red where his groin had been pink & gold   gorged by Idleroz's filed horns
soft rushes of the Guadalquivir   carried carnage   carnations   & cancions

Mannequins of boys & girls in First Communion dress   lined avenues of windows
one of the four who stand before God   Raphael was honored in monuments
soft rushes of the Guadalquivir   carried carnage   carnations   & cancions
though never singing the praises of the Mezquita   Góngora drank in its gardens

One of the four who stand before God   Raphael was honored in monuments
jasper   onyx   marble   & granite   856 columns were made in the hypostyle hall
though never singing the praises of the Mezquita   Góngora drank in its gardens
at bus stops from Seville to Cordoba   espadrilles displaced hard-packed sand

She heard two gusts of wind   leaves held her breath   but a wild rose blushed
in the grotto of Massabielle   a woman smiled at her   on the first apparition
Linda Darnell said "I am the Immaculate Conception"   in *The Song of Bernadette*
seeing no spring   the sickly girl began digging with bare hands in a muddy patch

In the grotto of Massabielle   a woman smiled at her   on the first apparition
enough water for drinking   bathing   & selling   possessed healing properties
seeing no spring   the sickly girl began digging with bare hands in a muddy patch
of those reported   67 miracles have been validated by the Lourdes Medical Bureau

Enough water for drinking   bathing   & selling   possessed healing properties
on 11 February 1858   Bernadette was gathering scraps of wood with her sister
of those reported   67 miracles have been validated by the Lourdes Medical Bureau
an incorruptible   she still looked 33 in a glass casket with wax on her face & hands

On 11 February 1858   Bernadette was gathering scraps of wood with her sister
only her crucifix showed signs of deterioration when her body was exhumed
an incorruptible   she still looked 33 in a glass casket with wax on her face & hands
she heard two gusts of wind   leaves held her breath   but a wild rose blushed

October   in the 5th & 6th arrondissements   poets prowled the boulevards
Baudelaire walked from his former home on the Île de la Cité   to his place of rest
everyday fresh flowers were left   for *the monarch of clouds   the cripple that once flew!**
over sewers   & beggar girls   towards the bracelet of barges on the Seine

Baudelaire walked from his former home on the Île de la Cité   to his place of rest
it seemed fitting to bring a syphilitic rose   or a bottle of Chateau Lafite Bordeaux
over sewers   & beggar girls   towards the bracelet of barges on the Seine
Paris reigned supreme   in literature   painting & photography   until WWII

It seemed fitting to bring a syphilitic rose   or a bottle of Chateau Lafite Bordeaux
filmed in the elevated windows   a lunch of baguettes & cheese   on the metro
Paris reigned supreme   in literature   painting & photography   until WWII
Oscar's penis was hacked off of Epstein's monument   & used as a paperweight

Filmed in the elevated windows   a lunch of baguettes & cheese   on the metro
the cold stones of the dead at Père Lachaise served as tables   Piaf the most beloved
Oscar's penis was hacked off of Epstein's monument   & used as a paperweight
October   in the 5th & 6th arrondissements   poets prowled the boulevards

*Charles Baudelaire

Mick's makeup was perfect   behind a yellow   chiffon veil   in Piccadilly Circus
Goats Head Soup had just been released   in the windows of every record store
a goat's head floated in a bowl of red soup   until eyeliner & lipstick was applied
the previous Sunday   Hyde Park heat removed everyone's shirts & blouses

Goats Head Soup had just been released   in the windows of every record store
it was the only album on view   since The Beatles left the studios on Abbey Road
the previous Sunday   Hyde Park heat removed everyone's shirts & blouses
"How unreserved," I thought, *Only mad dogs & Englishmen**   out in the midday sun

It was the only album on view   since The Beatles left the studios on Abbey Road
The Death of Chatterton   Rothkos & Turners at the Tate   made the world dissolve
"How unreserved," I thought, *Only mad dogs & Englishmen*   out in the midday sun
a suicide at 17 by cyanide   he was a beautiful forger of medieval poetry in his attic

The Death of Chatterton   Rothkos & Turners at the Tate   made the world dissolve
like the potted palms at Biba   on Kensington High St.   I fell getting off the bus
a suicide at 17 by cyanide   he was a beautiful forger of medieval poetry in his attic
Mick's makeup was perfect   behind a yellow   chiffon veil   in Piccadilly Circus

*Noel Coward

FROM KNOCK OF NEW YORK

*Murmurs of Leviathan he spoke   And rum was Plato in our heads** as the waters rose
a flock of prehistoric birds   flew up the East River   to every port & pier
white sails   refilled our glasses   on the Brooklyn Bridge   water music spilled
from Brian Eno's *Another Green World*   drowned in the slips   of cathedral spires

A flock of prehistoric birds   flew up the East River   to every port & pier
I bought an orange Bicentennial souvenir   no lettering   just a blue clipper ship
from Brian Eno's *Another Green World*   drowned in the slips   of cathedral spires
*I'm not that good at time anymore**   however   as t-shirts go   it was a masterpiece

I bought an orange Bicentennial souvenir   no lettering   just a blue clipper ship
after two Cuba Libres   the South St. Seaport smelled of salt tides & hot dogs
I'm not that good at time anymore   however   as t-shirts go   it was a masterpiece
something to cherish   long after the lovers swallowed enough of each other

After two Cuba Libres   the South St. Seaport   smelled of salt tides & hot dogs
in a heat to do so much   *O Stamboul Rose   dreams weave the rose**   interminably
something to cherish   long after the lovers swallowed enough of each other
Murmurs of Leviathan he spoke   And rum was Plato in our heads   as the waters rose

*Hart Crane

Tell me something I can hold on to   something to fill empty space   a star name
sold as white wine   it tasted like piss   say something over this bad excuse
CBGBs spelled cut glass in four letters   transcendence is a thirteen-letter word
I used to go to see my friends   break guitar strings   in ripped jeans & t-shirts

Sold as white wine   it tasted like piss   say something over this bad excuse
most bands were unaware of REM sleep   all they knew were needles & Heineken
I used to go to see my friends   break guitar strings   in ripped jeans & t-shirts
Patti's *Horses*   & Television's *Marquee Moon*   were in love with French Symbolism

Most bands were unaware of REM sleep   all they knew were needles & Heineken
I stayed until they started lobbing bottles at the audience   what was the point
Patti's *Horses*   & Television's *Marquee Moon*   were in love with French Symbolism
someone caught a tear in my eye   & walked me home to Bleecker & Elizabeth

I stayed until they started lobbing bottles at the audience   what was the point
the music was grounded in three chords   of Bowery flooded gutters & graffiti
someone caught a tear in my eye   & walked me home to Bleecker & Elizabeth
tell me something I can hold on to   something to fill empty space   a star name

The Empire State Building was a girl's best friend   the spring of unraveling
in the north window of the bridge to the building's rear   Manhattan blessed me
in a blue serge suit   Mac Dougal St. sold pizza slices   well past midnight
under the moon of Our Lady of Pompeii   I carried a white ship's napkin

In the north window of the bridge to the building's rear   Manhattan blessed me
a simple craft   unmoored   drifting on homeless   azure   sidewalk storms
under the moon of Our Lady of Pompeii   I carried a white ship's napkin
rained in by angel hair   through the nights   I wrote a hardcore detective poem

A simple craft   unmoored   drifting on homeless   azure   sidewalk storms
subletting   a turquoise & pink kimono from San Francisco   to block the daylight
rained in by angel hair   through the nights   I wrote a hardcore detective poem
it was essential for a woman to derange her senses   so Rimbaud had implied

Subletting   a turquoise & pink kimono from San Francisco   to block the daylight
Hammett & Chandler   duked it out   neither of them landing a solid punch
it was essential for a woman to derange her senses   so Rimbaud had implied
the Empire State Building was a girl's best friend   the spring of unraveling

He was an avid sailor   but he couldn't swim   facing the ocean in a topcoat
I'm addicted to coffee   I need it on a daily basis   or I will die   Please help me*
I left my bathing suit at the apartment   in May 1976   space soundly conspired
in The Metropolitan Opera House   *Einstein on the Beach*   broke through the ceiling

I'm addicted to coffee   I need it on a daily basis   or I will die   Please help me
whoever I went with   it's not relative   nor was the pink   portal-opening bird
in The Metropolitan Opera House   *Einstein on the Beach*   broke through the ceiling
for four acts in five hours   the incline of the upper balcony   was paralyzing

Whoever I went with   it's not relative   nor was the pink   portal-opening bird
had Einstein been beside me   he would have stood up   & stretched his legs
for four acts in five hours   the incline of the upper balcony   was paralyzing
1234   123456   solfeggio syllables   simulating mathematical splinters of glass

Had Einstein been beside me   he would have stood up   & stretched his legs
luckily   synthesizers   woodwinds   & human voices   kept me from falling
1234   123456   solfeggio syllables   simulating mathematical splinters of glass
he was an avid sailor   but he couldn't swim   facing the ocean in a topcoat

*Albert Einstein

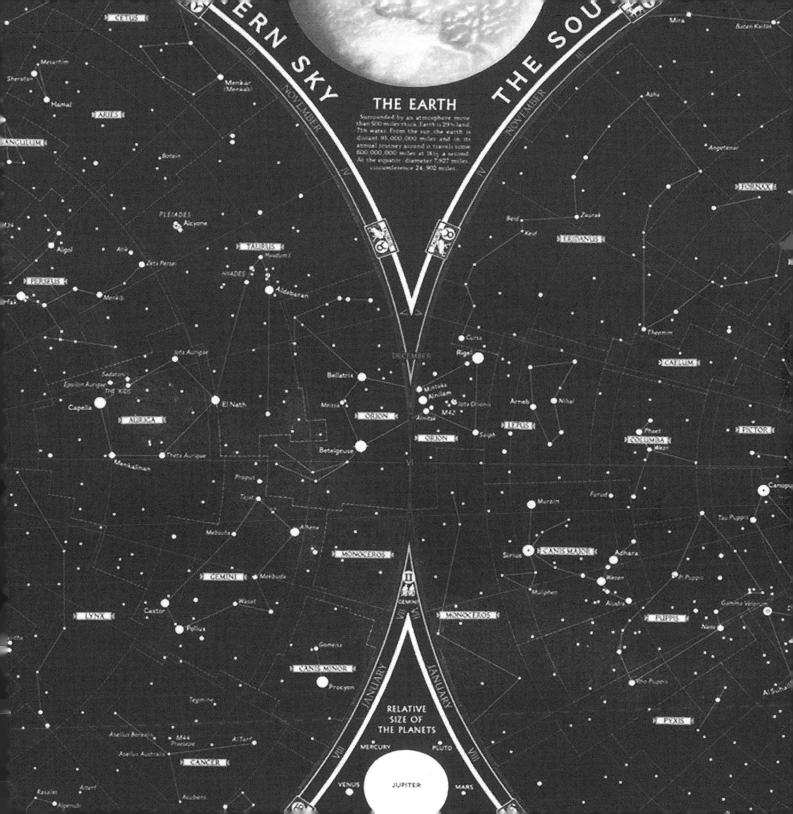

THE EARTH

Surrounded by an atmosphere more than 500 miles thick, Earth is 29% land, 71% water. From the sun, the earth is distant 93,000,000 miles and in its annual journey around it travels some 600,000,000 miles at 18½ a second. At the equator diameter 7,927 miles; circumference 24,902 miles.

RELATIVE SIZE OF THE PLANETS

from *REAL FIRE*
(2017)

The phases of fire are cravings and satiety.
                    —Heraclitus

REAL FIRE

Real fire is the central anthem calling birds to free themselves from tapestries.
Real fire has a secret known only to the confederacy of first-born super nova.
Real fire is a signal torch carried into the future by the children who nobody leads.
Real fire burns its bridges to impede the orchestra conducted by the rain.
Real fire is a slip of a girl dancing in a window before the bloody phalanx at dawn.
Real fire lays down its weapons at night to worship brittle trees and high grasses.
Real fire leaves its mark in the roses clinging to every balcony in the poet's city.
Real fire resurrects in cycles of five hundred years from the ashes of ancestors.
Real fire knows neither dignity nor pride when courted by the angels of the wind.

FIRE CANTO

The moths were so big they had faces. I heard
the universe charging at my back. The light principle
was so winded. In collapsing it gave birth to new life

I heard the blood pulsing in the stars. I heard
the grinding teeth of titanium. I heard the night chanting
rain, rain, rain. Simulating the lapping of water
against my walls. I heard the sheer numbers
of the night. In its dark belly a desperate rhythm of sleep

So forgive me for walking away with the flame

Everything is in order. Everything is in place. Animal tracks
stop at the door. Logs and kindling. Paper and matches. Maladies
work out in the red artillery pushing and pulling wings to different ends

Of folios buried deep in the sky the fire speaks. As long as it's fed
bones of skeletal rain jingle and jangle on the cabin roof

This is not an enraged aviary. Constellated in the northern woods
the birds attest to an all-forgiving eye. For hours and hours
they set off sparks. Spelling the names of the flames that gave them flight

A PURE BLUE INTELLIGENCE

From a comet you must have come
      –bringing with you two blue flames from the tail.

      That's where I lived. In the basin of ancient moon craters.
I learned to ride your porcelain horse.   In and out of star patterns
in your eyes
      –a pure blue intelligence sparked and flared.
      –fast, then slow like love.
      –stored in the trunk of an ocean liner.

From the birth of a heavenly body you must have come
      –bringing with you two rings of blue dust.

      That's where I lived. A moth in a white dress
hurling herself at the flame
      –fast, then slow like love.

Your pure blue intelligence was a steady source
      –bright enough for all the light needed to gather fuel in the forest.

SOLAR FOOTPRINTS

i

Every event and need should be a worship   seeing blessings take shape
in shadows   the sun makes reparations with the fire in our bellies
mercy and consolation   light is daily collected and preserved in lamps

ii

Along the Phoenician coast   papyrus was processed and dried in strips
books accumulated   sparks amassed   future fingerprints of scribes
lost their identity   on the indelible surface of the sun

iii

Look to the birds of the sky dismissing ordinary time   the clock face
of the sun is an iridescent disk of glass   pronouncing a liturgy of the hours
witnesses acquaint themselves with the past tense of brightness

FLAME

In search of the cause   ghost horses ride blindfolded into the fire

Roses   red carnations   poppy fields   the earth flourishes

People clear the land   unpredictably   the village is destroyed   sacred precincts shelter injuries

Shining torches astonish tigers   stepping out of the forest   the night's hallowed century

Gazing into the fire   concentration is important   the beginning holds the seeds of all that follows

Bodies open in consummation   rubbing together   everything that gives light has something to which it clings

Freed of vanity   nature ascends in radiance   from the funeral pyre

In search of the curve ghost horses die

blindfolded into the fire Roses reincarnations Poppy falls

the gentle flourishes People clean the land unpredictably the village is

destroyed sacred precincts shelter injuries Shining torches astonish

tigers stepping out of the forest into the moonlit hallowed century Gazing into

held the seeds of all

the fire concentration is important the beginning

that follows Bodies open in conversation rubbing

together everything that I was light has something to what it

clings Freed of vanity nature ascends in radiance

From the funeral pyre

METROPOLITAN

Pressing against glass   so it would pass
the car made its way
up Metropolitan   pieces of newsprint
under a magnifying lens
taking a beating from the sun   like everyone
I was a passenger   at the end
a building burned
in the rearview mirror

Some days you and I go mad   hearts break   minds snap

Snakes coiled in the sky   looking for means
to gauge statues in multitudes
in the windows   nameless shepherds
of the trees of the hills
wheeling through cross streets
and chain link lots   lying in wings
on star-grazed stone
the fear at the back of my throat

We can't go the old way   so we change   our lives pivot

Pages open to psalms of ache
on either side of the avenue
variants of old heavens   through wrought iron fencing
cold   colorless   marble   angels
with sculpted curls   came down
from their plinths   and guarded vaults
to douse the flames
in my eyes

Some days you and I go mad
Hearts break, minds snap.
We can't go the old way, so
we change.   Our lives pivot
forming a mysterious geometry.

FIRE WORSHIPPERS

As told to Viola Cooper, Professor, Oriental Studies, London University, at the Parsee Temple, Madras, India, 1937

Outside the monsoon rains come down but the fire is safe. The shadows of the flames dance on the walls. It's quiet here and dry. The roof of every house leaks. But the temple tiles are sealed. The fire burns. The flames dance and cast a glow - orange in the rain, yellow when the sun pours through the windows, distant planet red at night.

The fire first came to the people when a piece of star broke off and fell to earth. One woman was awake to witness the sliver slice through the darkness. It landed on the sand where she stood - a small rock with spokes radiating from the core like petals of a brilliant flower. The burning piece was so hot it singed the hair on her legs. She watched the petals jump from the rock to a bush to a thorn tree, which was dressed with the light of a thousand stars. That night the woman's excited cries alerted the people. They came and stood in awe of the fire. They gave it a name worthy of its wonder. Scrub brush was gathered to keep the piece of burning star alive and where it fell the first altar was erected.

The coming of fire changed everything. The people could light the interior of their tents at night and cook their food. They began to shine more brightly, feeling at one with the sand, the sky, the sun and the stars. The fire brought an elevation of spirit and sharpness of mind not previously experienced.

Inspired, the people invented metallurgy and made lanterns and bowls for fire altars. They invented an alphabet to record theories on the nature and origins of fire. Scholars wrote books addressing questions aroused by the arrival of the fragment of star: Was fire an embodiment of the divine? Why had it chosen such a form? What was fire made of? Was it the soul of the sun glimmering through pin holes in the dark? Had it originated in the distant red planet? Was it a strand of high-ranking seraph's hair cut off in battle? Had it been sent from camps in the high desert? Why were certain spices, gums and perfumed woods its favorite offerings? Why did it favor thorn trees? Were lions, horses and eagles made of fire?

So many books were written a library had to be built. For its location a valley in the steep foothills of the holy mountains was chosen. Scholars turned their backs on desert life and made a permanent camp around the library. The first temple, a building even larger and more beautiful than the library, was built for the burning fragment of star. In time the encampment grew into a city.

To bring in each New Year, a Festival of Fire was held in the city. People came in great numbers from the desert. They set up tents and stayed a fortnight. They dressed in white – the color at the tips of flames before they disappear into the air. During the day they fasted and prayed. They made offerings of incense and red petals in the temple. They visited the library to hear the latest investigations of the scholars. At night they celebrated. They visited each other's tents and ate elaborate feasts. On the last day the women torched thorn tree branches from the burning fragment and captured the flames in lanterns to bring back to the desert.

One year when the people were assembled for the festival strangers rode into the city. They shouted at the people from high mounts. They said the divine was invisible and only an ignorant people would worship fire. They stomped their boots on the camp fires outside the people's tents, but the flames resisted. They ordered the people to throw buckets on their fires, but the people refused. The strangers attempted to storm the temple, but the people created a barricade that held firm. In fury the strangers ransacked the library.

After a day of pillaging, the strangers were exhausted. The people cleverly blew the thick smoke of poppy gum into the strangers' faces and put them to sleep. That horrible day all the books in the library were destroyed. Many people were injured, but no one was killed. The people knew the strangers would eventually wake up. They also knew their wit was no match for the ferocity and numbers of the horsemen. So they broke camp. They tied their belongings to the backs of their camels. They retrieved the burning piece of star from the temple. They encased it in a brass lantern to protect it from the wind and they left the city.

Never stopping, they headed east across rivers and mountains. The journey was difficult. For those who had become accustomed to life in the city it was wrought with hardship. The scholars, especially, did not fare well. Only the hardiest nomadic people made it to the final destination, and upon arrival, more than half of them succumbed to diseases bred by tropical heat and humidity.

Now the monsoon rains come down and the desert is a distant longing in our hearts. Still we do our best to practice the old ways. Though this land is impoverished, we are safe. The local people worship strange gods, but they are agreeable. They leave us alone. We've kept our language. We've built a temple and a temple school. In recent years the school has even produced a few scholars, and after many generations in this hot, wet place, we're building our first library.

In three months' time we will have the Festival of Fire. Everyone will dress in white. Each family will come to the temple with a lantern. From the burning piece of star the women will take a flame. They will put it in their lanterns to protect it from the rain. Then they will return to their homes with fresh bundles of thorn trees and start the hearth fires for the New Year.

As a descendant of the woman at whose feet the first fire fell, it is my responsibility to gather the fresh supply of thorn tree branches for this year's festival. Without thorn tree branches the New Year can't begin. To collect the branches it's necessary to travel to the only region where they grow - the region of the holy mountains outside the old city. Since the people fled, the city and the surrounding lands have been occupied by the angry worshippers of an invisible deity. They have given the city a name of their choosing. To us it is an unspeakable name.

Tradition calls for me to make the journey with a band of women. It is a dangerous undertaking over a harsh terrain to which the people are no longer accustomed. Some have left not to return. For those who make it to the region, their lives depend on not being detected. Before we leave we will make offerings of spices, gums and perfumed woods. We shall pray that the fire in its benevolence accepts our offerings and ensures our safety.

L' UNIVERS
    for Rimbaud

You wear a ball on your shoulders! That's what you wear
of what it is composed. Unaccountably. Into
thin air it goes. Spinning on a spout of firewater
I spit out there in the lead. Land and sea
emblazoned on a blueprint. The preamble to my hell
O Seasons!   Bookshelves can't accommodate the leagues
I travel. Fore-and-aft. Sails and rigging
caught in motion in the clouds. Rail lines linking
white hot countries where fevers fester in the bones
even as I sit here. *O Castles!* The equator has my neck
in a noose. So get drunk!   Be sloppy! God damn
the stains on your shirt fronts. Tell them I shot you
while the constellation of my wounded boots
swam the crystal prisms of a glass of wine

XI

A red-tailed hawk on the windowsill of my heart.   Where
will it come from?   The last fire forever. The chandeliers swaying
in the apses of the chambers. Seeds from cranial pods in furrows
plowed by a chariot. The last fire forever.   Where will it come from?
the last brands in hollow stalks brought down from a brittle blue forest

The awakening sun as a red-winged lion.   Where will it come from?
the last fire forever. From the friction of silence and discordant music
the petals of a burnt poppy. When will they open?
the sleepless eyes. Mirrors reflecting daybreak at its peak of reddening

Where will it come from? The last fire? When will the small go away?
the condensation of melancholy go away?   The tips of the flames?
when will the last become an invisible vibrating tone forever?

SPARKS

i

A glint of light on the edge of a knife.
      –Does it herald a slit in the canvas
      –Or part the gates for invasions?

My happiness is aroused each time I catch a spark.

Is it my duty to never raise my head?
      –To lie down in fields of high grass?
      –To always carry matches in my pockets?

iii

On fair weather days, the birds on the canvas ignite. Finches
and pheasants become warm, glowing sparks, contained.

On fair weather days, the cloth of the canvas
has the weight of tapestry. It comes down from the wall
as a jacket. An enclosure of birds.

War, invasion, cruelty kept at bay.

–I'm invisible in the high grass to whomever rules
the world.
–I'm invisible. In an enclosure of birds.

vii

The light in the lantern is perpetual.

    The spark retreats into its private world.
    —It quiets itself.
    —It keeps to its personal quest.
    —It eliminates distractions.

    Whenever the wick burns down to the end,
love comes. The love of a friend, sensual love,
another seeker.

For all its need to be alone, the spark would die without love.

viii

Sparks are things with feathers. They take flight
from palazzos. From splendid cities of gold, red, white
and blue. They defy gravity with the lightness of thought.
     –Thoughts of ascending forever.
     –Thoughts of fidelity and loyalty.
     –Thoughts of free passage through the elements.

Predators look for light. They look for goodness. They shoot the sparks out of the sky.
They retrieve them where they fall and digest them.

Calm cruelty that comes so easily.

ASHES

Some nights ashes lay the ground   unseen   the divided shrine
bones   and scattered relics   a bundle weighing a thousand years
on the lawn   afflicted passions rub their bellies
in the four cardinal corners
what sense does it make   to start an argument
when the beginning is calling

*

Some nights are piles of aromatic kindling   waiting to ignite

Sweet bird   flushed with arrival   how high can you fly
in a life span   a ready nest is built
flame up   in desert crimson
shitting seeds to multiply   coded letters on the stars

*

Unseen   serrated blades   torn shirts & and dresses   dry as dust
the vestige of a swollen heart
hear now the last blood stones set in tiles   on the echoing green
spider veins   outlining   canyons too deep
to cross on a sighing bridge

*

Some nights are cords of symphonic timber   waiting to be torched

Sweet bird   flushed with arrival   how high can you fly
in a life span   a ready nest is built

Flame up
flame up
flame up

THE PARTING HOUR

There came a tremor   through the aisles   of Sunday afternoon

Rushing desert wind   saddle bag bells   camels on the carpet
in the living room   They said   be not afraid of waiting in the lowlands
where the grey skies attend   be not afraid of the conflagration   on the sofa
in an open book   be not afraid of cities lit from within   of stallions standing in blood

There came a tremor   through the aisles   of Sunday afternoon

They said   the tongue is a gift   for melting sailor's hearts   speak
to them of archipelagos   where the sun collects in mirrors setting fire to ships
of atolls   where the incense-breathing moon unlocks her doors at night   bones
in solemn stillness   wild white seas   to cross unaided

There came a tremor   through the aisles   of Sunday afternoon

Watch for the parting hour   the finishing stroke   the red wet petals
coming down   venom and its antidote   an open hand to the peaceful rain

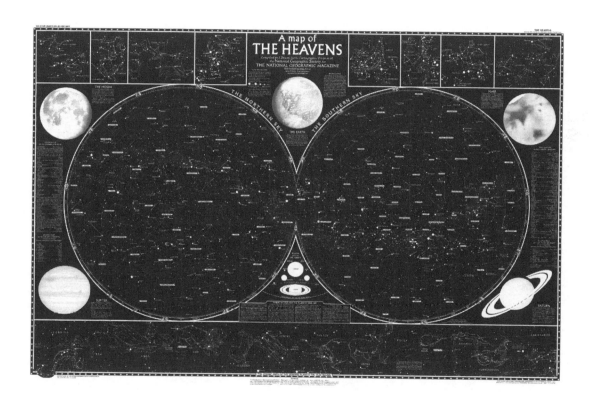

Notes

Real Fire is a collaboration with photographer Richard Baron 1948-2018. *Real Fire*'s, cover photograph and all the interior photographs are by Richard. The poems "Sacrifice" and "A Change of Skin" from *The Temple* (Telephone Books, 1980), each appear in this collection for the first time with "endings" written at least twenty years after the original body of the poem to extend the poems in performance with the band Moving Star. Lyrics "Rain" by: John Lennon and Paul McCartney. Copyright © 1966 Sony/ATV Songs LLC (Renewed). All rights administered by Sony/ATV Music Publishing, 8 Music Square West, Nashville, TN 37203. All Rights Reserved. Used by Permission in "Rain" from *Lost Ceilings*.

ACKNOWLEDGEMENTS

This book would not be possible without the dedicated publishers of the independent presses that have printed my work (in some cases more than once). I am fovever grateful to Craig Anderson (Oliphant Press), Maureen Owen (Telephone Books), Lee Ballentine (Ocean View Books), Bob Holman (Bowery Books), Tod Thilleman (Spuyten Duyvil) and Tamra Carraher (Alexandria Quarterly Books). I'd also like to thank Peter Carlaftes and Kat George of Three Rooms Press who published my collection of short fiction, *Tales from the Eternal Café* (2014). "Autumn Melancholy," p.60 and "Fire Worshippers," p.190 were included in that collection. *Troublante* was printed in a limited edition of one hundred copies. Its contents are reproduced in their entirety in this collection. A number of poems first appeared as limited edition broadsides—"The Big Sleep," p. 17, appeared as a broadside illustrated by Neil Winokur; "Subterraneous," p. 20, was first published as a broadside illustrated with a stock photo of statues from Mesapotamia; "Hotel Rabat/Sleeping Fit," p. 22, was published as a broadside, illustrated by Ken Tisa; "Sleeping Gypsy," p. 104, was first published as "Madam Bogart's Arts of Animal Ecstasy, illustrated by the author; "The Enigma of Buster Keaton," p. 127, was published as a broadside/pamphlet illustrated with a still from Keaton's silent film *The Frozen North*; "Byron's Time Sheet," p. 140 was first published as a broadside with an authentic time sheet watermark; and "He was an avid sailor but he couldn't swim facing the ocean in a topcoat," p. 176 was published beside Maureen Owen's "standing on the pedals keeps you nimble from the very top of envy half of the people burn ultraviolet or where did May Kasahara's letters go?...or had he received them…it seemed he had…" in a broadside illustrated by Jane Dalrymple-Hollo.

There are so many friends and family members to thank for their endless support and encouragement. Without their help, I might never have left the starting gate. Thank you Patti, Michael, Cath, Bob, Cyn, MO, Trid, Tom, Adrian and, especially Joe.

JANET HAMILL is the author of eight collections of poetry and short fiction. Her work has been nominated for Pushcart Prizes and the Poetry Society of America's William Carlos Williams Prize. *Tales from the Eternal Café* was named one of the "Best Books of 2014" by Publishers Weekly. A strong proponent of the spoken word, she has performed at The Poetry Project at St. Marks Church, The Walt Whitman Cultural Center, the Bowery Poetry Club, the Knitting Factory, CBGB's Gallery, the Nuyorican Café, Central Park Summer Stage, Lowell Celebrates Kerouac, the Andy Warhol Museum, Seattle's Bumbershoot Festival, the Liss Ard Festival in County Cork, Ireland, Patti Smith's Meltdown Festival in London, the Latitude Festival in Southwold, England, and Liverpool's Heartbeats series. She was one of the first poets contracted to Mouth Almighty Records and has released two CDs of spoken word and music in collaboration with the bands Moving Star and Lost Ceilings—*Flying Nowhere* and *Genie of the Alphabet*. A documentary about the creative process of Janet Hamill and Lost Ceilings, directed by Bryan Hamill, *Bearing Witness*, is viewable on You Tube.

Hamill has been a writer-in-residence at Naropa University, a teaching assistant at New England College and an instructor at Cabrillo College. She has also lectured and taught workshops at the Poetry Project, the College of Poetry, the Seligmann Center, the Goshen Library, as well as clubs and galleries in London and Liverpool.

After residing in NYC for three decades, Hamill moved to New York's Hudson Valley, where she founded and directs the teaching/reading series MEGAPHONE.